Praise for *The*

For some grandparents "play" does ___
others, it's their natural gift. No matter which type of grand you
are, *The Gift of Play* delivers just the right amount of inspiration
and education to help all grandparents understand and joyfully
practice this essential part of their grandchildren's early
childhood development.

Christine Crosby, Editorial Director, GRAND Magazine

As a geriatrician, I know that for many older adults who are
grandparents, the time spent with their grandchildren is the
most important part of their lives. Judith Van Hoorn's *The Gift
of Play* combines expert opinion about developmental changes
in children with delightful vignettes of real interactions.
This book will be so helpful both to people anticipating their
future grandparenthood as well as those who already have
grandchildren. The practical tips about the importance of close
family relationships are among the highlights.

Barrie Raik, MD, Geriatric Medicine
Weill Cornell/New York Presbyterian Hospital

In *The Gift of Play* Dr. Judith Van Hoorn explores the mutually
beneficial aspects of play for grandparents and grandchildren.
Not only is there joy on both sides of the equation but also the
bonds that are strengthened and the skills that are developed by
young and old are significant. Play offers the perfect environment
for exploration, creativity, language development, emotional
support, love, and sheer delight. Dr. Van Hoorn discusses the
myriad benefits of play with a unique respect and awe for what
the play relationship between grandparents and grandchildren
offers. Parents and grandparents should read this book. It's a gift
from the author.

Mary Bevernick, President, Global Grandmothers

This engaging book describes the importance of play for both social and intellectual development and offers great tips for grandparents.

Jeffrey B. Gould, MD, Professor in Pediatrics
Stanford University Medical Center

Grandparents from different cultures may play with their grandchildren in different ways. But one thing is universal: the exquisite delight that arises from such playful encounters. This book captures this creative joy. Its universal appeal to grandparents around the world comes from stories of happy moments and skilled insights that teach with a light heart. I look forward to giving my fellow grandparents a copy of this book!

Christine Montiel, Professor Emeritus
Psychology Department, Ateneo de Manila University

Can you imagine what it feels like to a child to have a grandparent (or any trusted adult) engage in mutual play with delight? Judith Van Hoorn's new book encourages grandparents to recognize the joy for all in playing together. A myriad of possibilities and first-hand accounts support even the most timid grandparent to explore the delights of playing with children.

Suzanne Di Lillo, Retired School Principal and Head Start Director

In *The Gift of Play* Dr. Judith Van Hoorn uses delightful narratives of grandparents to describe the co-creation and re-creation of mutually beneficial spontaneous play in relationships of grandparents with their grandchildren. This book celebrates the reciprocity that develops in these relationships and the contributions grandparents' play can make to the multidimensional development of their grandchildren. Dr. Van Hoorn offers many exciting examples of various types of spontaneous play that adults who read this book will be drawn to explore with young children.

Corann Okorodudu, Professor Emerita
Developmental Psychology and Africana Studies, Rowan University

Judith Van Hoorn's book *The Gift of Play* should be required reading for all grandparents, both new and seasoned. Beautifully written and illustrated with charming stories of loving grandparents and their grandchildren, this book is not to be missed.

Dr. Van Hoorn, a grandmother and professor emeritus of education and psychology, writes from both perspectives. Her understanding of child development allows her to delve deeply into all aspects of young children's growth. Her experiences as a grandmother inform her understanding of the strong ties that bind grandparents and grandchildren. Dr. Van Hoorn explains in a very readable way how grandparents can support their grandchildren's cognitive, social, emotional, and physical development through playful interactions that are fun for both grandparent and grandchild.

Blakely Bundy, grandmother and Co-Director of Defending the Early Years

This book is a delightful dive into aspects of play between grandchildren and grandparents. It is beautifully written and informative. Our play repertoire with our two grandchildren far away in Germany will certainly be enhanced.

Judith Standley, Nurse-Midwife, and Andrew Standley, Diplomat

The Gift of Play is an excellent addition to my grandparenting library. As grandparents, we get a second chance to be young again when we play with our grandchildren. This book celebrates play and offers a wealth of ideas to inspire play with our grandchildren.

Donne Davis, Founder of the GaGa Sisterhood

With insights, ideas, and stories about how play enhances the lives and development of children, this book is a terrific resource for grandparents wanting to add to their repertoire of fun things to do with their grandchildren. Opportunities abound within its pages for creating magical moments for all concerned.

Steven Gallon, Behavioral Health Consultant and grandparent

The Gift of Play

How Grandparents Enhance the Lives of Young Children

Library of Congress Cataloging-in-Publication Data has been applied for.
Subjects: LCSH:
Grandparenting. | Grandparent and child. | Family. | Play. | Child's play. | Development, Child.

ISBN 978-1-7360971-0-6

First paperback and ebook edition February 2021.

Cover and layout design by Amy Reff | FreelanceAmy.com

Photo credits: Grandparents and parents contributed 32 photos and gave legal permission for their family photos to be used anonymously without photo credits. Other photo credits include: p. 77, 123RF/Cathy Yeulet; p. 96, iStock.com/Aldomurillo; p. 160, iStock .com/Anna Frank.

Printed in the USA.

Judith Van Hoorn
grandparentplay@gmail.com
judithvanhoorn.com

*To the grandparents whose stories,
wisdom, and photos enrich each chapter.*

And, always, for Derek and our grandchildren.

Table of Contents

THE GIFT OF PLAY

Foreword

The Gift of Play: How Grandparents Enhance the Lives of Young Children is a warm invitation and a welcome promise for grandparents. Both the invitation and the promise are richly fulfilled as each chapter unfolds. Author Judith Van Hoorn is well known as an expert on play, having been a familiar voice for teachers of young children about the essential connection between play and learning. Here, in her newest book, she takes up with tender vignettes and irresistibly persuasive evidence another relationship—the compelling relationship between grandparent and grandchild at play.

The invitation is, quite simply, to play. The book makes the case for finding the time and way to play with grandchildren because play can do much for our youngest generation—from anchoring daily fun and special festive traditions to becoming a beloved elder friend and confidante. But the message goes much deeper. It outlines specifically what playing with grandchildren can do both for the grandparents themselves and for their own children, who are on the joyful but challenging journey of parenthood.

I have worked for many years in the field of early childhood. For me, *The Gift of Play* is a revelation, an inspiration, and it has a message I will long carry with me. Here is what I learned and re-learned from this book: I was reminded that play encourages connections that are life-giving to children, and that as a grandparent I can focus in ways that can benefit all generations in the family. Stories of other grandparents' playful experiences helped me expand my sense of all that play can be and all that is possible, helpful, and appropriate in my family. *The Gift of Play* is deeply and purposefully a book about love—the love between the child and the grandparent, heads side by side, hearts full, knowing that whatever happens, together they can create a safe harbor, for a time short or long, when they accept the invitation to play.

I am a grandmother to four. We have lived together sometimes, lived far apart at others, gathered for joyous family traditions, faced loss together, watched over a preemie in an incubator, and toilet trained twins. I wish *The Gift of Play* had been in my hands throughout the early days of grandparenting. This book has invited me into a role that is unique in my experience—one of encouragement, acceptance, respect, and celebration.

In the book, we meet the grandmother who dances with her little ones, feeling a freedom she never experienced when she was a mother. We also learn how to make full and regular contributions to memory-making while being a grandparent at a distance. There are practical suggestions, but this is not a *how-to* book as much as it is a *why-do* book. It is part story book, part developmental explanation, of what can happen when, for example, we bake together with our grandchildren. *The Gift of Play* is not about giving recipes—grandparents know what flavors and treats will delight in their family—but why the habit of getting out Grandpa's mixing bowls and stirring the ingredients makes such a difference to a child. The stories are real-life experiences that may inspire, parallel, or augment those of the reader.

This book speaks to grandparents from many diverse cultures, circumstances, and life paths. It promises them all that within their reach is the capacity to keep trying, to continue to connect with grandchildren playfully as they grow, to imagine the mind of the child, to return to the ways and days when we loved to play with passion, abandon, and intense commitment.

Becoming a grandparent is a navigation with ourselves as we answer the question: What kind of grandparent will I have the opportunity to be? Van Hoorn helps us answer that question with the encouragement to play our way into becoming someone who understands the child deeply, respects grandchildren's preferred ways of learning and being, and enhances those hours and days when we have the privilege to be together.

Elizabeth Morley
Principal Emerita, Dr. Eric Jackman Institute of Child Study
Laboratory School, University of Toronto
Visiting Scholar, Kobe Shinwa Women's University, Kobe, Japan

CHAPTER 1

The Gift of Play

Paula and her grandchildren, three-year-old Brianna and five-year-old Cooper, are dancing to music from the 60s. It's time for *Sgt. Pepper's Lonely Hearts Club Band*. Paula brings out a penny whistle, a child's drum, and a few wooden spoons the children like to bang together to mark time. They march energetically around the living room. Cooper then leads the merry band around the dining room and out onto the patio. When the music stops, Brianna exclaims, "Play it again, Grandma!"

Outside in the late afternoon, Nick stands under the mulberry tree with Marcus, his 10-month-old grandnephew. Sunbeams reflect off the leaves. The sun hangs low in the sky, half hidden behind the tree and casting shadows against the fence. Moving shadows of leaves on branches flit across the fence. As Nick moves toward the fence, Marcus reaches out to touch the shadow leaves. Nick does the same. Silently, they touch the dancing shadows with their fingers.

Play is at the heart of relationships between grandparents and grandchildren. Many stories we tell about our grandchildren convey our joy in all the ways we play together. Pretend play, physically active play, nature play, blocks, puzzles and board games, songs and stories, everyday and special occasions, inside and outside.

This book is an ode to the gift of play, a celebration of the play between grandparents and grandchildren. Inspired by the joy my husband Derek and I have playing with our grandchildren, it features dozens of stories in which grandparents and honorary grandparents share their delight in play.

This is not merely a how-to book with activities for young children. As you read it, I hope you will find many new ideas, tips, and practical information to enrich your play, as I have found while writing it.

I've studied and written about young children's play since the 1970s when I was a mother with young children. Then, little had been written about young children's play. Happily, there are now hundreds of resources for parents.

Today I look at play through the eyes of a grandparent. Unfortunately, what remains missing—despite the growing popularity of grandparenting books, blogs, and articles—are books about the joy and importance of play. *The Gift of Play* aims to help fill that gap and celebrate play among grandparents and grandchildren.

Research supports the multiple and often parallel benefits of play for older adults and for young children, such as improvements in physical vitality, emotional well-being, social interactions, thinking abilities, and creativity. Play is essential for grandchildren and grandparents—and playing together magnifies its power.

Play enriches our grandchildren's lives and our own. Whether you're a new grandparent or a grandparent with years of experience, I hope this book will deepen your understanding of the importance of play and give you ideas for expanding your repertoire. The very nature of play makes it powerful in enhancing close and loving relationships. Grandparents want to love and be loved, and playing is a special time to feel and express love. We play because play is fun for our grandchildren and fun for us—and playing with those we love is special.

The Benefits of Play

We know from our own experience that parents have great responsibilities, busy lives, and often not enough time to play. Yet young children need lots of time to play, especially time for spontaneous, unstructured play that promotes their curiosity, imagination, and creativity. As grandparents, we can give our grandchildren the gift of play, and when we play with our grand-children, both children and families benefit.

Throughout this book, I discuss how play (which our grand-children love to do!) supports their development and learning. As we play with our grandchildren, we can support their social and emotional development, imagination, creativity, thinking abilities, language development, strength, and physical abilities. Each chapter emphasizes one of these dimensions of play while showing at the same time that all play is multidimensional.

The gift of play is a gift for ourselves as well. Playing with our grandchildren makes us free to be creative and inventive. It provides the respite and energy we need for renewal. Play is a time for us to revel in spontaneous fun and recapture our childlike sense of wonder.

This is a book about families. We bequeath and enrich our family heritage when we show by example that generations in our family play together—throughout childhood, adolescence, adulthood, and then grandparenting years. As grandparents, we can purposely promote playful traditions for our grandchildren.

Elaine told me this story:

Cooke and I have four grandchildren; Audrey and Sydney
live nearby, and Tommy and Benjamin live a long day's drive
away. We take care of four-year-old Audrey and eight-
month-old Sydney several days a week.

I was taking care of Audrey on a warm summer day, a perfect
day to have some pretend play at the park and have a picnic,
too. We packed the car with what Audrey decided we'd need
for a picnic and for the babies (her stuffed animals and dolls)!
Tenderly and carefully, she "clicked" the babies into their car
seats. I drove to the park with her specific directions. "Mimi,
go straight ahead and turn right at the corner. I hope there's
not a traffic jam!"

The Gift of Play highlights the strong traditions of grandparent and grandchild play. Each of us plays in different ways.
I draw from my observations and conversations with dozens of
grandparents across the U.S. and from several other countries.
Some grandparents see their grandchildren often. Others find
creative ways to grandparent remotely or virtually because of
distance, emergencies, or health issues.

Each chapter includes insights from experts on young
children's play, development, and learning. The anecdotes,
stories, and discussions in the chapters reflect both the diversity
of grandparents and the diversity of play. How fortunate we are
when we can play with our grandchildren!

Why We Play with Our Grandchildren

Although theorists and researchers speculate about why people play, few ask the players. No one, it seems, has asked grandparents. When I asked grandparents, I found that they answered at length without hesitation:

We play just for the fun of playing. It makes him happy.

Playing games makes kids laugh.

When we play, she's becoming a loving, affectionate person.

It strengthens her arms and legs, and she's learning to balance herself.

He learns to give and receive love and affection.

He's communicating even though he's so young.

We play together—and they learn who we are.

When we play together, we witness their fast-paced development, their creativity, their interests.

Comments like these reflect the multiple reasons grandparents like to play. It's no wonder that many grandparents and grandchildren can spend hours playing together.

During these conversations, some grandparents said that they play with their grandchildren in much the same ways they used to play with their children. Others point out that they're with their grandchildren for shorter periods of time than they were with their own children, so they postpone other things they need to do. As grandparents, they feel more relaxed and playful than when they were parents.

What Do We Mean by Play?

Watch young children even for a short time, or think about the stories in this chapter, and you'll see that play takes countless forms. There's play that children initiate and play that adults suggest. There's large muscle rough-and-tumble play, nature play, and play involving language. There's play in which children explore, pretend, and play with toys.

Sometimes play has simple rules, like Simple Simon or Candyland. More often, children's play is open-ended and spontaneous with endless creative possibilities. We see children playing with dolls and cars or building with blocks. We see children run and dance, draw and paint, sing and clap their hands. The list goes on.

What is play? Is it play when you cuddle with your grandchild and read a favorite picture book? Is it play when you take a walk and your grandchild looks for worms? We need a definition of play that's expansive, one that includes all the activities grand-children and grandparents do to have fun together.

You might assume that a book about play would have a commonly agreed-upon definition of play. Not so. Play is easy to identify but difficult to define. But my conversations with grand-parents and my research convince me that all of us know what we mean when we use the word "play." Ask young children what they're doing and they often reply, "I'm playing."

Writers from fields like psychology, education, anthropology, and philosophy have tried to define the term fully. The challenge is to come up with a definition that includes all the myriad types of play, from young children's spontaneous rough-and-tumble play to strategic games like chess. The definition would apply to all forms of play across developmental ages, cultures, and even history. That comprehensive definition of play is elusive and remains to be written.

Instead, researchers identify characteristics of play. I find that the following characteristics occur most commonly in grandparent and grandchild play. Which ones in this list describe your own experiences?

- Children and adults are having fun with one another.

- They're focused and actively engaged.

- Their play is spontaneous, with no rigid rules.

- Their play is voluntary, with no need for reward. They play because they want to, and either one can decide to stop.

- For both children and adults, the process of playing is more important than achieving a specific goal.

Play between grandparents and grandchildren is characterized by the fun we have and our delight in one another. We take our cues from our grandchildren and become attuned to what pleases them. Though we sometimes take the initiative, our purpose is mutual pleasure. When our grandchildren grow older, our play becomes more truly mutual as they, in turn, learn what delights us, makes us smile, and keeps us engaged.

When people play, they signal to each other that "this is play." With babies and toddlers, we often smile and open our eyes wider. Especially among preschoolers and kindergartners, play often includes pretending. Grandparents may notice that young grandchildren are still learning the concept of rules and when they apply. So when they play games, they can't yet follow defined and fixed rules. For younger children, rules are flexible, they may be forgotten, or new rules are declared: "No, Grandma, now we play it this way!"

Another characteristic of play is the age difference between the players. When we think of preschoolers, school-aged children, or teenagers playing, we often imagine them playing with friends their age. The most common exception is play within families where we see people of different ages playing together. And, with grandparent and grandchild play, the age difference is usually the greatest.

What might that mean for grandparents in terms of what we play and how we play? To begin with, we have to adapt our play styles to one another. For example, we need to update our repertoire of songs, stories, books, and movie plot lines, and definitely update the names of popular superheroes and princesses.

I'm also keenly aware that while my grandchildren's physical abilities are growing, my own abilities are declining. It's increasingly challenging to deal with the physical limitations I didn't have when my own children were young—or even when my oldest grandchild, now 19, was little.

All of us grandparents are learning to adapt to this new situation. Sometimes I'm physically exhausted after a day of taking care of two active grandchildren. Indeed, one day at the park, after I'd spent a long time pushing my then four-year-old granddaughter Ava on the swing, I explained that I needed to rest a moment. Ava looked up at me. "It's OK, Grandma," she said patiently. "Take as much time as you need."

I find that play among grandparents and grandchildren generally continues for extended periods but alternates with other activities. Sometimes, we flit back and forth between play and caregiving activities such as feeding our grandchildren. Caregiving can be rushed. We might need to change an uncomfortable diaper quickly or rush to dress a child for preschool. In contrast, play and laughter cannot be hurried. So, even when playful times are short, they remain relaxed and cherished moments.

Play Connects Generations

Play is a golden thread that connects all of us as one human species, across continents and cultures. Play connects each generation's traditional, but often unseen, heritage.

Play Is Our Family Heritage

What memories do you have of family play, of playing with your parents, grandparents, sister, brother, or other relatives? Singing, storytelling, joking around, bingo games, building with blocks, or frisbee in the park? What kinds of play connect the generations in your family?

Many grandparents remember playing with family members. They specifically mention playing with their own grandparents. Some are happy to remember growing up in a family that played a lot. As she talked with me about playing as a child, Suzanne recalled, "One of my great memories and models was seeing my grandparents play. They had card parties and croquet parties and danced and told stories and jokes and recited poetry. I always knew play was not confined just to children."

Others have loving memories of their grandparents but say their grandparents were serious or that times were hard so people didn't play. And others say they treasure their opportunities to play with their grandchildren because either their own grandparents lived far away or they never knew them.

Old photos sometimes remind us of playful intergenerational connections. We might see how our own parents or grandparents held us close and smiled in just the same way we hold and smile at our own grandchild. Perhaps we remember playing a game of checkers with a grandparent on a rainy day.

Now as grandparents, we may pause as we play peekaboo, recalling a similar moment when we played with our own baby. We might remember how this infant game developed into hide-and-seek and later into a game of tag. Perhaps we see glimpses of our own parenting replayed as our son tells a bedtime story to his child, the next generation.

In fact, even when we don't consciously remember, play may be woven into a family tradition that shows us that *how* we play, as well as *what* we play, is passed on subtly to the next generation. It could be the specific way we hold a grandchild, or the playful tone we use as an invitation to play, or the way we stand as we show a grandchild how to throw a ball.

Sometimes memories return unexpectedly. As I lace up my granddaughter's skates, my daughter Alia says, "I remember the fun of skating when you spun us around."

Play Is Our Cultural Heritage

Anthropologists, psychologists, and educators write that cultural practices of raising children are passed from one generation to the next: "For me, playing this way is cultural." "Growing up we all played soccer." "When my daughter was born, I called my mom in Mexico and asked her to tell me the words to Pon" (a Mexican baby game).

Six-year-old Elijah races excitedly down the field, practicing soccer with his grandfather Aart who is visiting from the Netherlands. When they take a break, Aart notes how much more skillful Elijah has become since Aart visited last year. He remembers back to when Elijah was a toddler and how they'd roll a beach ball back and forth.

Jason's grandmother, Popo, tells me that the following baby game reminds her of playing with her grandmother in China.

Popo sits on the floor, her feet outstretched, balancing Jason on her lap. She holds his wrists and he holds her thumbs as she rocks him back and forth to the rhythm. She smiles and they gaze at each other as she recites the words:

搖到外婆橋	*Row, row, row to Grandmother's bridge.*
亜婆話我好寶貝	*Grandmother says I am a good baby.*
又比糖,	*Grandmother gives me candy.*
又比餅	*She gives me cookies.*
打鑼打鼓	*She beats the drum and gong merrily*
送返來	*To accompany me home.*
問爸爸好不好	*Grandmother asks if Daddy is fine.*
問媽媽好不好	*Grandmother asks if Mama is fine.*
Jason說都很好,	*Jason says, "They are fine, they are fine."*
都很好	*After Grandmother hears it,*
外婆聽了咪咪笑	*She is happy and smiles.*

Popo says that she loves to imagine this happy scene and picture the grandmother beating the drum and gong merrily. For Popo, songs and games are part of the heritage she wants to pass on to Jason.

My own professional interest in play grew out of my early memories of playing with my Grandma Goldie and watching her play with my younger sister and cousins. Goldie had emigrated from Russia in 1904 with few physical possessions, but she brought many lullabies, stories, and children's games. The baby games she played with us were mostly in Yiddish. Now, with my own grandchildren, it feels special when we play those games, like the little clapping game we play with babies that my grandmother called Potche, Potche Kikhelekh.

Potche, potche kikhelekh	*Clap, clap little hands*
Mama machen zekelekh	*Mama will make socks*
Papa macken shikhelekh	*Father will make shoes*
Far da klena kindela.	*For the beautiful little child.*

Note: This is the version I remember. There are many variations depending on where families lived. My mother's friend provided this transliteration from Yiddish years ago, but there is now an accepted standard system.

In my research for this book, I found no formal studies of grandparenting and play. But wherever I see grandfathers, grandmothers, and grandchildren in the real world, I see play. I am convinced that how we play, as well as what we play, reflects our culture as well as our family. There are still so many unanswered questions for future research. Do grandmothers and grandfathers play differently? What languages do we use? How does our play change with grandchildren's ages?

Play Is Our Human Heritage

Because we humans play, we have been called *Homo ludens* (the playful species) as well as *Homo sapiens* (the wise species). Theorists and researchers write about play as a universal human activity, seen not only across cultures but also across time, as found in ancient artifacts around the world. Developmental scientists consider play particularly important in the early years. And though play is a particularly dominant activity during childhood, it is also part of what makes us human across our lifespans.

Playing with Grandchildren: A Wealth of Possibilities

The play of each grandparent and grandchild has its own distinctive style, rhythm, and repertoire that changes as children grow. Think of Paula and Nick whose stories introduce this chapter. When grandparents play with infant grandchildren, they're exquisitely in tune with what pleases the infants. As grandchildren become preschoolers and then kindergartners, play times grow longer and become more collaborative as children learn what delights their grandparents, makes them smile, and keeps them engaged.

> Ava loves to invite us, her grandfather and me, to join her for nature walks. When we're outside, we're captivated by the way she shows us lots of "nature" around her neighborhood. Last spring, she showed us the tiny flowers blooming by the curbside and the light green leaves just unfurling on the mulberry tree. In summer, she ran ahead to find dandelions so we could blow and scatter the seeds. Sometimes she remembers to take her magnifying glass, perhaps to count the legs on an insect or show us the tiny stamens on a flower. Now in autumn, we take leisurely walks, engrossed as we collect leaves of brilliant colors, acorns, and dried flower seeds. Ava brings along a little paper bag for her nature treasures so they don't get broken in her pockets—or washed.

Play happens anytime and anywhere—sometimes in surprising places. Jim recalled taking his grandson Owen to the pharmacy to pick up a prescription. The line was long and they waited for ages. Jim was feeling tired when Owen reached for his hand and asked whether the pictures he saw on the tissue boxes were also on the tissues inside. Jim answered that sometimes tissues inside did have different colors, but he'd never seen one with pictures.

All of a sudden, Jim felt like they'd entered a story: "If we could get ones with pictures, that would make runny noses fun! I'd get ones with animals—maybe a cheetah that runs fast. What about you?" Owen answered he'd like dinosaurs. "Then," Owen continued, "if you sneezed, my dinosaur would surprise your cheetah!"

Recently, I met my neighbor Rosie playing at the park with her one-year-old granddaughter Isa:

> Rosie "runs" after Isa, calling, *"Corre, corre, ve!"* ("Run, run, go!"), then turns and "runs" the other way. (Actually, while making a dramatic show of running, Rosie is purposely moving very slowly.) Isa looks at her and vocalizes what sounds like *"cor, cor"* and then turns and toddles after her grandmother, moving as quickly as she can while holding onto a picnic bench for support.
>
> Seeing Isa's trouble balancing, Rosie affects great excitement, drops onto the grass, and begins crawling. Immediately, Isa plops down and crawls excitedly after her grandmother. What a fast crawler—she catches her grandmother quickly. They hug and Isa chortles.

As they played, I realized their play had so many facets. Loving, fun-filled interactions, mutual communication and understandings, and physical activity that may have challenged Rosie as well as Isa. And all of this was taking place in a park where Isa was outdoors in the fresh air, feeling the grass, seeing the trees and bushes, and hearing the exciting sounds of many children playing.

The chapters that follow both confirm the importance of grandparent and grandchild play in building loving relation- ships and explain how play supports children's development and learning. Though each chapter focuses on a particular aspect of play, all chapters show that grandparent and grandchild play is fun and multifaceted. The final chapter, "The Gift of Play Continues," celebrates the joy of playing with our grandchildren throughout their childhood and into adulthood.

CHAPTER 2

Loving Relationships

As grandparents, we want to love and be loved by our grandchildren. We show love in so many ways. We cuddle our little ones, sing lullabies, and play peekaboo. We show our love for our preschoolers and kindergartners when we curl up together to read a book, play at the park, or pick them up from school and share a snack together. And for many, love means virtual visits or traveling long distances to be with their grandchildren.

We want to feel loved by our grandchildren. We're thrilled when a newborn relaxes so completely in our arms, when a toddler cuddles up against our shoulder as we read together, when a preschooler races to greet us when we arrive, or when a kindergartner draws a picture of us walking hand in hand.

In the past few years, I've spoken with scores of grandparents and others who are active grandparenting figures in a child's life. They live in different areas of the U.S., from the East Coast to Hawaii, and several other countries. The amount of time they spend with their grandchildren varies tremendously. Many see their grandchildren several times a month. Some take care of the children every day or several times a week. Others miss seeing their grandchildren in person and find creative ways to feel connected virtually.

In these conversations, we talked about what contributes to close, loving relationships. I asked specifically how they liked to play and whether—and why—they thought play creates loving relationships. This chapter features quotes from these conversations to highlight grandparents' wisdom about loving relationships and the importance of play.

Developing Loving Relationships

No matter how much time they spend with their grandchildren, all grandparents told me about how loving relationships develop as they do ordinary things in affectionate, loving ways. Benina, a grandmother of four, talks from her years of experience:

I think it's the predictable, steady things and little routines that really contribute to building close relationships, like what I call our "Grandma and Hiro" time. I used to pick him up from preschool every Tuesday. We'd go to a coffee place where he had his special hot chocolate, the one they made so it wasn't very hot. Now that he's a kindergartner, we still have our regular time together and he likes doing other things. I think about what he might remember, what will contribute to his life story.

Grandparents who live farther away send cards and gifts for special occasions, but most emphasize they feel closest when they interact with their grandchildren during virtual visits or see them in person.

We keep in touch often by phone. When we visit, we can't wait to give the little ones a little snuggle. We think it's important to point out how they're growing, changing, and doing different things. For example, I might point out how much better they're doing something now than last time. Whether we're talking on the phone or visiting them, we always tell them—our children, grandchildren, and great-grandchildren—that we love them.

From birth ...

From when she was born, I wanted to see Hannah frequently and be in her "inner circle" so I might really help out in a hands-on way. I made sure to be there often, so she'd get used to me physically—see me, smell me, and so on. I focused on comfort and familiarity. I wanted her to get used to me as an everyday person, so she wouldn't be surprised to wake up and find me there. If she was a little on the cranky side, I wanted to be able to calm her. When I'm with her, the rest of the world doesn't matter. From when she was born, I wanted Hannah to experience pleasure that would grow into love.

... to later infancy ...

My nine-month-old grandson always wants to be outside. He loves nature and loves watching people. So that's what we do. We're lucky to live in Hawaii where we can be outdoors all the time. We sit and cuddle, and watch people walking by or gardening or building something. He loves being at the beach. Last Sunday our whole family went to the beach, all four generations. He got to play with everyone in the sand and the ocean. Together, we watched his older brother and cousins swim, surf, and play volleyball on the beach. I'm so lucky—his first year is so precious.

... and throughout the early years.

We care for our grandchildren several times a week. They're two and four. We want to be hands-on grandparents, day-to-day grandparents. They know we're part of the family. The kids say, "There's Mama and Daddy, and Mimi and Papa." Love is a visceral feeling. So many things we do are kinesthetic—lots of hugging, touching, cuddling. Our grandson Ellery sleeps at our house several times a month. He comes into our bed in the morning and there's always lots of tickling, talking, laughing, and jumping on the bed.

Play and Loving Relationships

Playing is a special time to feel and express love. The very nature of play enhances close and loving relationships. Play is different from the other things we do. We play because play is fun for our grandchildren and fun for us—and playing with those we love is special.

How does play enhance love between grandparents and grandchildren? The other chapters in this book highlight dozens of stories grandparents have shared with me. Any of these stories would serve as an excellent introduction to this chapter on play and loving relationships.

Let's revisit two stories from the first chapter. Both show that grandparents and grandchildren bring their own styles to the way they play. At the same time, all their play shares basic characteristics. Everyone enjoys being together and having fun. Notice that Paula and Nick are focused, engrossed, and devoting their full attention to their grandchildren. They're unhurried. No pressure to rush. No phones to check. Like partners in a dance, they tune into their grandchildren's rhythms and energy.

Paula and her grandchildren, three-year-old Brianna and five-year-old Cooper, are dancing to music from the 60s. It's time for *Sgt. Pepper's Lonely Hearts Club Band*. Paula brings out a penny whistle, a child's drum, and a few wooden spoons the children like to bang together to mark time. They march energetically around the living room. Cooper then leads the merry band around the dining room and out onto the patio. When the music stops, Brianna exclaims, "Play it again, Grandma!"

Outside in the late afternoon, Nick stands under the mulberry tree with Marcus, his 10-month-old grandnephew. Sunbeams reflect off the leaves. The sun hangs low in the sky, half hidden behind the tree and casting shadows against the fence. Moving shadows of leaves on branches flit across the fence. As Nick moves toward the fence, Marcus reaches out to touch the shadow leaves. Nick does the same. Silently, they touch the dancing shadows with their fingers.

Play times are perfect moments to be exquisitely observant, sensitive, responsive—times to delight in one another. Times to have fun. Indeed, as researchers point out, these characteristics are typical of all good play with young children.

Grandparent-to-Grandparent Advice

Throughout our conversations about building close loving relationships, grandparents gave advice from their own experiences.

As grandparents we give our grandchildren our focused time and patience. Compared to parents, we're more free to play. Think about the developmental level of your grandchildren and do what they like. Mostly, you want them to see your genuine smile and the way that you're just beaming pleasure.

Grandparents view their grandchildren as the next generation of their family. They know that strong, healthy relationships with the parents will contribute to developing a loving relationship with the grandchild. Nurturing and respecting both generations, those of parents and grandchild, further strengthens family relationships overall. Grandparents want to contribute to family happiness and harmony, to be there for their children and grandchildren—even when they can't be "there" physically.

> *Be very aware of family connection. Make sure you're not in any way competitive with the parents and their role. You need to support their connection with their children.*

> *From the beginning, it was important to follow what my daughter wanted from me—it felt lovely to do what the new parents wanted.*

In these conversations, the importance of intergenerational relationships was particularly emphasized by several great-grandparents.

> *You always have to think of building close relationships within the whole family. This is especially important for us since we live far away from our children, grandchildren, and great-grandchildren. We want close relationships to continue across the generations. I had a close relationship with my granddaughter when she was a child even though she lived far away, and we didn't see her often. We maintained this strong connection as she grew up. Now that she has little children, she encourages them to feel close to us. We love our video chats when we get to see what our great-grandchildren are doing.*

> *Everyone in our large family loves my mom, their great-grandmother. Everyone wants to spend time with her. She always tells us, "The way to spell love is T-I-M-E." She and my dad were teachers in the Philippines before our family moved to the U.S. Some of the little games they play are*

teaching games, like "Where is your nose? Where are your ears?" But most of all, they encouraged all their children and grandchildren to be imaginative, creative, and, above all, enjoy being together as a family. My mom is in her 90s and she's not very mobile anymore. She still makes little homemade dolls for her younger great-grandchildren, and they love playing together. Now I'm a grandmother and I'm trying to keep these traditions I learned from my parents.

Grandparents as Practitioners of the Art of Play

I think of grandparents as practitioners of play. Some have recently become grandparents and are looking forward to many years of play. Others have been grandparents for many years and have lots of practice, often hundreds of hours spent playing with grandchildren. *In either case, I think grandparents aim to be expert practitioners of the art of play.*

Watching and listening to dozens of grandparents has led me to deeply admire what they do—what we do—and how we play. It was natural to turn to other grandparents for their insights and advice about how playing with their grandchildren builds loving relationships.

Play is what little kids want to be doing all their waking hours. To the degree that your interactions don't include play, it's a distraction from what they want to do. You want to do what's fun for them—it's fun for you too because of the joy it brings them.

I'm more relaxed than when I was a parent. I have the luxury of time. I want to do things that are fun. I'm thinking, "I'm going to focus on you."

Grandparents shared with me their wisdom about how play builds loving relationships. With their varied perspectives and wealth of experiences, other grandparents give us much to think about.

Play makes bonds stronger. When you play, showing affection is part of the package! Kids have fun with you. You make them laugh and they make you laugh. Our grandkids know what we like to do, and that we have different toys and books at our home that are fun for them.

I think that lots of time together builds love, especially time spent playing. When you play, you're giving your grandchild your undivided attention. They can feel that you think they're important. For instance, the other day I picked up Ellery from preschool. He said he wanted to go out for a walk and then go together to get some food. I thought that would be fun, so I told him: "That's exactly what I want to do!"

Play is something kids enjoy a lot, and they relate to whomever they play with. I think the sharing part is a really big thing. Sharing the things you enjoy with someone contributes to your closeness.

From infant to toddler to preschooler and kindergartner, children's play changes dramatically during the first five years. Play reflects all aspects of children's rapid development—physical, emotional, social, cognitive, and linguistic.

Play changes over time, changes to be age appropriate. Especially when they're babies, you cuddle a lot and you play silly games, surprise games like peekaboo. Later, you cuddle and read. As they get older, there's pretend play, like playing with dolls and building things with blocks and Legos. Physical play changes too. When they're young, you do a lot more just flinging them about, tossing them in the air. Physical play gets different. They like different kinds of things, like climbing or playing with a ball, and I enjoy these things too.

It can be reassuring to know that as children grow older, the ways they show feelings of closeness and love may change as well. Elaine explains that her five-year-old grandson is not as physically affectionate with her and her husband as he used to be. His interests and skills have broadened, and he is often actively engaged, more independent—no time for hugs and cuddles. They've learned that naptime, quiet times, and bedtime are more likely times for him to show physical affection.

Grandparents are keenly aware that children's play reflects their individual preferences as well as developmental changes. One sibling prefers sitting at the table, happily paging through a picture book, drawing, or doing puzzles. The other wants to be out on her scooter or running down the block with you.

My sister Leni pointed out that we grandparents, too, have our favorite ways of playing:

We all have things that we prefer. Personally, I love reading to them, playing in the park, playing in the sandbox. I don't love all aspects of play. I wouldn't choose to spend my time building with blocks or Legos or playing board games. But I love building my relationship with them through play, so I do it because they love it.

At any age, grandparents and grandchildren have fun discovering playful activities they both enjoy, whether they live nearby or visit virtually. Dennis smiles as he tells this story and reflects that play promotes love in both directions.

Charlotte's five. She loves making silly faces and loves it when I make silly faces, too. I got the idea of using my phone so we could take photos. I take photos of her making silly faces and she takes photos of me. Great fun!

Several grandparents explained it's reassuring to remember that play is not always conflict free although conflicts occur less frequently when it's an activity they're both enjoying. They watch to see if their grandchild is still involved or if their interest is waning. At times, they find the activity seems dull because it's their own interest that's waning!

Conflicts are more likely to occur at certain times for certain kids, perhaps when they're tired and cranky, or when they get up from a nap, or when they want to do something that the adult thinks would be unsafe, or when they just need the chance to "let the wiggles out." Then we know it is usually time to change gears. We needn't wait for conflicts to escalate before we respond.

Of course, as Linda pointed out, it's not only about our grand-children. "You need to be flexible. Even if you have an activity in mind, you can't be rigid. In fact, if a grandparent has a plan and decides 'this is the way,' that's what leads to conflict."

Chandra talks about working out compromises between the child's desires and the grandparent's understanding of what is safe or healthy. "For example, when it's raining and my 20-month-old granddaughter says she wants to play outside, I tell her, 'When the rain stops, we can go outside. We can't go outside now. We have to stay inside till it stops raining. What do you want to do?' I think I'm also teaching her that I'll follow through on my promises."

Sometimes, what first appears to be a conflict turns out to be a misunderstanding. Grandparents find that misunderstandings occur more frequently when children are eager to express themselves but are difficult to understand. For example, children may have trouble communicating when they are just learning to talk or have delays in their speech development.

We get to care for Sydney (20 months) on Mondays and Tuesdays. One late afternoon, she was playing on the floor getting restless and in an increasingly louder voice was demanding, "Watch Papa! Watch Papa! WATCH Papa!" I was busily chopping veggies for salad. I turned to watch her, "What do you want me to watch? Are you going to show me something?" She gave me a blank stare and went back to

demanding "WATCH Papa!" After a couple of anxious rounds
of this, it dawned on me she wanted to "watch Papa!" I lifted
her into her high chair, and she was fully satisfied to watch
me cook. She was happy that her sentence was (finally)
understood, happy that she got what she wanted, and
pleased with our "game of communicating."

Not surprisingly, when we're having fun doing things that we and our grandchild both enjoy, we often do it again and again until it becomes a familiar ritual. Several grandparents talked about what we might call "playful rituals." I find this concept useful. For instance, when Eduardo gets the text that his preschool grandchildren are about to arrive, he goes out to the porch and sits on the wide glider. Sitting on the glider serves as an invitation for them to join him and decide what they'll play.

Grandparents talked about how familiar play rituals helped maintain closeness during virtual visits, especially with babies and toddlers.

I find play rituals make things special. They're something
unique to you, that your grandchildren associate with you.
In this way you have more fun together. Rituals evolve over
time. With babies, rituals are often something physical like
finger plays or a simple chasing game. My granddaughter
Alma knows I'm the grandma who plays finger plays, so she
starts wiggling her fingers whenever she sees me on the
computer.

Mary talked about the familiar routine that helped her 20-month-old granddaughter Hannah warm up more quickly each week during their virtual visits.

I'll ask her if she wants to see my house. She always says "yes." I take her on her usual tour just as if she were visiting— the kitchen, her high chair, family photos on the wall, her toys behind the sofa, and of course, Ella, the elephant!

During the COVID-19 pandemic, there was a flurry of advice and tips for distance grandparenting. Distance grandparenting was nothing new for millions of grandparents around the world who had been grandparenting remotely or virtually for years, whether for reasons of location, health issues, or various other precautions. They are the real pioneers of virtual grandparenting.

The following tips are drawn from two articles I wrote during the pandemic. (See the Resources list at the end of this book for links to both complete articles.)

Tips for Making Play & Playfulness an Important Part of Distance Grandparenting

Experiment with these tips to see what works best for your family.

➤ Make virtual visits special times to focus on grandchildren. Plan other times for adult talk.

➤ Follow your grandchild's lead to make virtual visits feel more natural. Each child behaves differently online as well as offline. Some are always eager to talk—others prefer to listen or want to go off and play. It's helpful when parents and grandparents agree not to push young children to talk or interact with their grandparents during online visits.

➤ Use virtual visits as opportunities to continue family traditions like singing, dancing, sharing stories, and exchanging jokes with young children.

➤ Continue telling stories and reading together. Enjoy reading a book while a parent or older sibling carefully arranges a short picture book so you can read easily and talk about the illustrations. It's also fun to watch a parent reading a book and cuddling up with the child while you comment from time to time.

➤ Enjoy the simple pleasures of sharing food. Plan and coordinate a virtual snack visit—especially a snack you've eaten together in person.

➤ Send photos and texts that require less coordination with parents to share with your grandchild. Some preschoolers and kindergartners love replying to texts with their own string of emojis.

(cont.)

➤ Most important of all, don't be camera shy. Be the
grandparent your grandchild knows and loves. Be outgoing
or a quiet observer. Ask questions or tell stories. Sing and
dance around. Listen patiently to your grandchild tell a story.
Enjoy being silly together. Give yourself permission and go
ahead!

The Art of Play Is the Art of Attunement

Few grandparents are familiar with the concept of attunement,
or being in tune, which is a term often used by professionals,
such as educators and mental health practitioners, who work
with young children and their families. Yet attunement is implicit
in grandparents' conversations—and obvious when we watch
grandparents playing. So what does attunement mean and how
does it relate to play? I asked several education and mental health
professionals to talk about grandparenting, attunement, and play.

Dr. Dorothy Stewart, founder and director of the Old Fire
House Schools that are recognized for their focus on building
caring relationships, describes attunement in action and why it is
important for play:

You need to be attuned to play well with another person.
What does this mean for a grandparent playing with
their grandchildren? We think of attunement as nuanced

attention. For grandparents, that means you're paying close attention and responding to your grandchild's signals, their facial expressions, body, tone, and the way they move. You attend to their nonverbal communication as well as their verbal communication. For example, you might notice what they're looking at, how long they pay attention, and their tone of voice. Then you make your responses reciprocal, by looking at what your grandchild is looking at and mirroring the child's tone of voice.

Dr. Julie Nicholson, who teaches higher education courses on play and has written numerous books about young children's play, describes the cycle of attunement:

Grandparents have the unique opportunity and privilege to "notice" children's brilliance, and through their caring and attuned presence to reinforce to a child that they are loved. Whether an infant is exploring the sounds of a rattle, a toddler is learning how to use finger paints, a preschooler is donning a hat and trying out what it feels like to be a firefighter, play supports grandparents to express love in subtle and powerful ways ... by leaning in and asking a question, or carefully observing how a child uses materials, or responding to their grandchild's joyful smile or contagious laughter.

Play allows grandparents to express and strengthen their love through words, gestures, and emotions that communicate, "You are a gift to me and to us. You are safe and you belong. Exactly who you are in this moment matters to me." I see this cycle of attunement as beautifully displayed in the play between many grandparents and their grandchildren.

Dr. Mary Sickles, a child psychiatrist and grandparent herself, captures the feelings of attunement in play:

You're sharing an emotional moment. You're communicating your affection and sharing pleasure. It's genuine communication, genuine pleasure. You're aligning your emotions. You're feeling you're on the same wavelength— super-connected.

When we are attuned to, or in tune with, our grandchildren, they learn to attune to us. Attunement becomes mutual. Over time, children learn to pay close attention and respond to our signals, our facial expressions, movement, communication, and so on. They learn what we like to play as well as how we play.

Through play, young children gradually develop their ability to attune to others. As grandparents, we want our grand-children to "play well with others." Research shows that play contributes to children's emotional well-being as well as social abilities—confirming the wisdom of generations of grandparents. It's wonderful that all the while we're playing together and having fun, we're helping our grandchildren develop important social abilities so that they learn how to be a good friend, have friends, and have fun.

I find grandparents' stories particularly powerful because they show how truly attuned grandparents are when they play with their grandchildren—how they're exquisitely observant, sensitive, and responsive—and what delight they have with one another.

Play Enhances Close and Loving Relationships

➢ Play allows grandparents to express and strengthen their love through words, gestures, and emotions that communicate how much they love them.

➢ Sharing the things you and your grandchild enjoy contributes to closeness. Find activities that you and your grandchild both like. Play is about having fun together and delighting in one another.

➢ Devote your full attention to your grandchildren. Stay focused and tune into your grandchild's rhythms and energy. Relaxed, unhurried times enhance feeling connected.

➢ Play reflects children's individual preferences as well as all aspects of their development.

➢ Don't wait for conflicts to escalate before responding. Be proactive and flexible.

The following is one of the many stories that portray attunement. My friend Cooke, the Papa in this story, wrote about a special outing with his two-year-old grandson Benjamin. Cooke pointed out that the magic of one-on-one time is best found in simple *one-on-one* experiences taken slowly at the child's pace.

Benjamin and Papa had a foggy morning to spend together in the San Francisco Bay Area. Papa planned on a trip to a local kids science center located in a forested park along the San Francisco Bay. They arrived early so Papa decided to "kill some time," walking around before going to the "real deal."

Walking down the slope to the water's edge included a little slipping and sliding, and Benjamin loved the "adventure." The bay is the landing and takeoff zone for the very busy San Francisco airport, a very loud intrusion to the quiet foggy morning in the park. To Benjamin, however, each jet soaring close overhead elicited excited cries and finger pointing: "Airplane, airplane ... BIG airplane!"

In the brief breaks between the jets, Benjamin and Papa talked about the boats moored at the small marina, "Look Benjamin, big boat!" "Papa, big boat!" "Ben, look, big blue boat!" "Papa, blue boat!" "Papa! Papa! BIG AIRPLANE!!!"

After spending much more than what was planned as the allotted excursion time outside, Papa and Benjamin hustled into the kids science center. Benjamin was genuinely interested in the various kid-centric and hands-on visually and auditorily stimulating displays, but none elicited the rapture of the "BIG AIRPLANE!!" outside.

The time spent by Papa and Benjamin alone in the woods and by the bay was golden, much more so than the exhibits made to capture the attention of the children.

I wrote the following poem during the months we had to shelter at home during the COVID-19 pandemic. I was inspired as I reread the thoughtful, loving words I'd recorded from these conversations with other grandparents. And I thought about how much Derek and I missed Elijah, Zoë, Ava, and Jake and knew grandparents around the world were missing their grandchildren, too.

> *I love to be with you.*
> *I love to have fun together.*
> *I love to do what you enjoy.*
> *What's fun for you is fun for me.*
> *I hear your laughter and see the way your smile lights up your face.*
> *When the sound of my own laughter joins with yours,*
> *My eyes twinkle and crease with delight, and my crow's feet take wings.*

THE GIFT OF PLAY

CHAPTER 3

Grandparents, Grandchildren, and the Development of Play

As much as our past experience leads us to expect it, we never cease to wonder at our grandchildren's rapidly developing capacity for play from birth to age five. We marvel at the changes in their physical, social, emotional, cognitive, and language development. And, of course, the ways we play with our grandchildren inevitably reflect these changes.

Playing with our grandchildren is all about being in tune with them. I don't play with a "typical three-year-old" but with my grandson Jake. I think about what Jake enjoys and what he can do. I enjoy watching his abilities develop as he plays with his parents and his seven-year-old sister Ava.

This is a book about grandparent and grandchild play, so this one is not the typical chapter on child development we read when we were parents. Instead, I will talk about how grandparents' play relates to grandchildren's development in the first five years. I focus on us as *grandparents* and also consider how play reflects our own interests and experiences as well as our changing abilities.

This chapter is divided into two parts. The first is about babies and toddlers, from birth to about age three. The second highlights key developmental changes from age three through five. Feel free to decide whether to read the entire chapter for an overview of play during the first five years or just the section that interests you most. If your grandchild is a baby, I hope that reading the second part enhances your anticipation of playing together in the years ahead. If your grandchild is older, I hope that reading about the first years brings back wonderful memories.

Part I. Playing with Babies and Toddlers

Even as babies and toddlers, our grandchildren teach us how to play. We see a multitude of changes during the first years. As a researcher and now as a grandparent, I'm amazed at how the grandparents I've spoken with are so responsive to their grand-babies' individual development as they rock them, sing, tickle, clap, roll balls, and play peekaboo.

Some people might not connect a baby's first months with playful interactions. Grandparents learn from experience that just as it's important to read to young children before they are capable of reading, it's equally important to play with infants—though they're not playing as they will when they're older.

From birth, whether they are awake and alert or sleepy and irritable, our grandchildren guide us to adapt to their state of alertness. We learn when to slow or quicken our pace, when to continue, when to stop. Even in these first months, we tailor our play to respond to our grandchildren's individual differences in temperament, such as their activity levels, distractibility, the intensity of their reactions, and their attention spans. We observe closely to see what makes our grandchild content. We experiment and try to extend these precious moments.

With babies, we take the lead and support their early attempts to play, making it easier for them to participate. Early childhood educators call this "scaffolding." We scaffold young infants' play most obviously by physically supporting babies but also by what and how we play. Importantly, we help babies regulate their emotions by being careful not to overwhelm them.

Adaptation is mutual. Our grandchildren adapt to us as play partners, just as we adapt to them. As grandparents, each of us has a different touch, and each of us holds them a bit differently. Babies learn to adapt to how we position them. Sometimes they squirm around to be more comfortable, perhaps snuggling up closer to our body or withdrawing into our arms. They adapt to our tone of voice, our communication style, our rhythm, our play repertoire.

What makes all social play distinctive is the subtle communication that *this is play*. Think about how we communicate that we're playing. In these first few months, this important communication is markedly one sided. We smile more often and open our eyes wider and, especially with babies, check to make sure they're gazing back at us. We use a "playful" voice and speak in a higher tone, "Hey little one, let's see if you want me to rock you!"

Prelude to Play

Babies' very first months are a time of immense change and challenge. Newborns learn to adapt to differences among their caregivers, to distinguish our faces, voices, and even smells. They're also getting to know the sounds and sights of their environment.

When we're getting to know our grandchildren, we discover that play times are the perfect moments for us to be exquisitely observant, sensitive, and responsive to their changing abilities and interests. Sometimes, whether they're awake or asleep, we might see them smiling even though these are not the more social smiles they will develop in a few months when they smile back at you. What makes them content makes us happy. What a special time to fall in love again!

Our play with newborns is not like our social play with older infants, toddlers, and preschoolers. Still, it's definitely social play for us. We're actively engaged, motivated, energized, and having fun. What engages them engages us. Our play develops in sync with our grandbabies. As we interact gently and playfully, we watch to see if they're tracking our movements. Sometimes we see their interest conveyed through a prolonged gaze at our face.

> I'm sitting on the couch holding Jake, at this time three weeks old. He's more alert now that his mom has nursed him. I'm supporting his head and body on my legs. His sister Ava, four years old at this time, climbs up beside me. We both look down at Jake. "Hi, Jake—this is your big sister Ava."
>
> I look at him, then begin gently looming by gazing down at him and slowly moving my face toward him and then away. He gazes at me intently and follows my movements.
>
> Ava moves closer to Jake and catches his gaze. She moves back and forth, imitating my looming movements, delighted when he begins to stare at her. I sit motionless, watching this delicate early play between sister and brother.

At times I find it hard to read young infants' responses because their muscle coordination is not well developed. In fact, sometimes a baby's flailing arms and kicking movements actually signal their interest and pleasure. It's easier to interpret their responses a month or two later when they respond to social interactions with their appealing coos and gurgles.

Each week, we can see newborns develop new abilities. In these first months, play is all about the senses. From birth, the infant's world is already a world of sights, sounds, touches, smells, and temperature, as well as the kinesthetic sense of position and movement.

In particular, they're highly alert to the visual world. Newborns are nearsighted and see objects most clearly at about 15 inches. This is the very distance for them to clearly see our face when we hold them. In fact, researchers find that newborns prefer looking at faces, especially eyes, and often track repetitive movements. Look at grandparents' play. When I watch grandparents playing with newborns, I find that most playful interactions occur within this close distance, this intimate space. I notice that grandparents often play face to face and repeat their actions—like the baby game Ava and I played with Jake.

Even at birth, a baby's senses of touch, position, and motion are well developed, and researchers highlight the importance of these senses. Pediatricians recommend the same gentle interactions with newborns that grandparents around the world have passed down from generation to generation, like the way we carry and rock newborns so they feel our warmth and touch and move with the changing rhythms of our body.

Babies are keenly sensitive to human sounds, especially higher tones. For years researchers have written that mothers speak to babies using a higher voice, calling it "motherese." More recently I've read about "fatherese" and "siblingese." Let's add "grandparentese." Think about how we grandparents talk to our newborn grandchildren. We use higher tones as we sing to them, from traditional lullabies to the silly ditties we make up.

Over the years, grandparents have asked me questions about temperament, especially when they notice great differences between their grandchild's temperament and their own. I spoke with Dr. Ann Sanson, Honorary Professorial Fellow (Professor) at the University of Melbourne and lead researcher on the intergenerational Australian Temperament Project. Ann's explanation is reassuring:

> There is no evidence that differences in a grandparent and grandchild's temperament will have negative impacts on their relationship. Temperament is biologically based and is partly inherited but is modified from birth by the environment the child experiences. Temperament is thought of as a building block for later personality. It tends to be moderately stable over time, but not unchangeable— modest change is more typical. For instance, a highly reactive grandchild is unlikely to become the most laid-back adolescent but may become less reactive. A very shy young grandchild is unlikely to become "the life of the party" but may become less shy.
>
> Perhaps grandparents with young grandchildren might be more helpful to the child if they're aware of four dimensions of temperament, each along a separate continuum: activity, sociability, reactivity, and regulation. None is value-laden— that is, there are strengths and challenges associated with each. (See the Resources list at the end of this book for Ann's description of these four dimensions of temperament and the implications for grandparents.)

When infants are about three or four months old, the way we play with our grandchildren changes. Parents and siblings are playing differently, too. What's happening?

Developmental scientists describe striking changes in behavior that mark the end of the newborn period. Changes in play result from biological and cognitive changes. For example, the newborns' world broadens as their vision improves. At three or four months, they can look across the room and see people and objects more clearly than before.

Other biological changes include an increase in the number of brain cells and increased myelination—the thin coating on nerve cells throughout the body that enables more rapid transmissions along nerve pathways. These biological changes result in infants' faster physical responses.

For many of us, the most striking behavioral change is the appearance of a "social smile." Now, babies smile in response to the smiles of others around them—and smile so that we'll smile back. Researchers find parents are apt to say that their baby seems more joyful and that they feel more connected.

Does the same hold true for us grandparents? Researchers haven't yet investigated this question. But just watch us when our grandchild beams at us with rapt attention and shines that bright beacon of a social smile. And see how play starts to change.

Becoming Partners in Play

Infants become more playful between four and seven months old. Their play reflects not just their physical development but also their developing social and emotional, cognitive, and communicative abilities. Changes in how grandparents play reflect and support these changing aspects of babies' development. Now grandparents are playing peekaboo, clapping, tickling, and rocking games. Now it's time to bring out stuffed animals and dolls, rattles, balls, and large soft blocks.

Amparo holds six-month-old Luis on her lap facing her. His head is no longer wobbly, and he's able to hold it steady without support.

Amparo smiles at Luis and opens her eyes wide. She holds his hands and begins rocking back and forth. His movements are now more fluid because of his increased torso strength and coordination. They continue to rock in synchrony for several minutes while both maintain eye contact. Amparo repeats the verses to the game several times (lyrics below), and each time Luis responds with a smile. Back and forth and back and forth. What a sweet example of playful turn-taking!

Pollito frito	Fried chicken
Pollito asado	Roasted chicken
Para Papá que viene cansado	For Papa who comes (home) tired.

Amparo explains that she loves returning to the childhood games like Pollito Frito that she knows from Mexico. She speaks Spanish and English fluently, and wants her grandchildren to be bilingual.

Watching Amparo playing, we get an idea of new milestones in Luis's physical development. His bones have become harder and stronger and, because they can bear more weight, he can hold up his head without support. Amparo says that he's able to sit alone and is even beginning to crawl.

The nerves in the brain and body continue to develop throughout infancy, which means babies' physical coordination—needed for crawling—and their thinking abilities improve. Babies are learning a lot from their experiences although, obviously, we can't "see" their thoughts. At this age, they begin to anticipate the patterns of the repeated motions so characteristic of infant games as we play peekaboo or bounce them on our knees.

During these months, babies' social and emotional development is more rapid as they interact with more people. They become better able to recognize emotional expressions such as affection, joy, surprise, anger, fear, and sadness. And as our grandchild's range of emotional expressions increases, we grandparents become more sensitive to their emotions and more able to respond to their subtle cues. Grandparents find that play becomes more mutual toward the end of the first year.

Liam sits facing 10-month-old Chloë. Both are smiling and Liam is holding up the cloth they use to play peekaboo. As they look at each other, Liam playfully covers Chloë's face and asks, "Where did Chloë go?" Chloë pulls the cloth off her face and laughs. "There she is!" Liam exclaims with mock astonishment. Next, Chloë holds the cloth up to her face. Liam again asks, "Where is Chloë?" Chloë uncovers her face in delight as her grandfather exclaims, "There she is!" Both grin. Chloë then leans on Liam and pulls herself upright to standing, nods her head, then hands the cloth back to her grandfather. She's ready for another round.

Researchers find that appearance, disappearance, and a surprise reunion are elements that characterize games grandparents play in countries around the world, from the peekaboo games of early infancy to the hide-and-seek games of later childhood. We grandparents can celebrate another shared experience—all these games involve the same finale, which is the joyful reunion of grandparent and grandchild!

New Dimensions in Play

When we grandparents talk about toddlers, we generally think of children between one and three years old. This hasn't changed since our own children were little. What has changed is that pediatricians and early childhood educators pay more attention to the individual variation in young children's development. Look at a group of toddlers playing in the park. We notice differences in what they can do as well as differences in their height and weight. It's useful to keep in mind that there is great variation in grandchildren's growth and development.

Take walking. What about one child who walks independently at 11 months and another not until 15 months old? Should the family of the child who is 15 months old be concerned? It's important for children to have regular pediatric checkups that include developmental screenings and, especially, clear communication between families and health professionals. In this case, it will be reassuring for the family to know that walking at 15 months falls within the normal range. (See the Resources list at the end of this book for a link to information from the American Academy of Pediatrics website healthychildren.org.)

We play in tune with our grandchildren's unique rates of development as well as their interests and attention spans. Typical play like hide-and-seek, clapping games, and rolling a ball highlight the kind of developmental milestones we see in the transition to the toddler stage.

When we look back at photos from just five or six months ago, we marvel at how much our grandchild has changed and wonder what we'll see during the months ahead. Important physical, cognitive, and social and emotional development occurs during the toddler years and impacts the way toddlers play with us and vice versa.

Consider physical development. A baby's first steps look like balancing acts—legs wide apart and arms held out for balance. After toddling around for a few months, babies become better coordinated and more assured walkers. When we look at their body proportions, we find their bodies have grown larger relative to the size of their heads. Changes in children's body proportions as well as increases in the strength of their large muscles help explain the changes from crawling, to toddling, to coordinated walking, and later to running.

Ryan's parents call their neighbor Joan his "local grandmother" and appreciate her love and helpfulness. At 20 months, Ryan is definitely physically adventurous and social. Today, Joan has taken Ryan to the neighborhood park. She stays a few feet away so he can move about independently yet definitely close enough to make sure he can take risks but play safely.

Joan watches as Ryan goes up the taller of the slides, spirals down, then runs quickly to the smaller jungle gym where he climbs up and swings side to side on the bar, imitating the older kids he sees playing on the bigger jungle gym. He sits for a moment on the cement rim around the sand area, watching two older children playing on the grass with a foam soccer ball. Eager to play, he loudly calls out to them, "ba'ba ... ba'ba."

Fortunately, one of the other children, who looks about four years old, understands what Ryan wants to do and that he's trying to say "ball." He answers Ryan, "You wanna play ball?" Ryan nods and the boy walks over and gives the ball to Ryan. Ryan tries to kick the ball but misses. The older boy says, "Good try—wanna try again?" Ryan nods. The boy carefully places the ball directly in front of Ryan. Ryan kicks it. Success! It rolls in the general direction of the other child who runs, picks it up, celebrates by pumping a fist in the air, and exclaims, "Yay, you got it!" before running off to play with his friend. Ryan watches them for a moment and then runs back for another turn on the slide.

Toddlers can do so many new things. So much of toddlers' play also requires increased small muscle strength and hand-eye coordination as they scribble with thick crayons or assemble puzzles with large pieces or build with blocks.

At this age, we see new cognitive abilities emerge and others develop more fully. We might notice that our grand-child continues to look for a ball that has rolled out of sight or search for us when we play hide-and-seek. This shows that she is capable of symbolic thought, the ability to mentally represent objects—or people—that are not physically present. Symbolic thought is a major achievement. Linguists find that toddlers' increased understanding and use of language generally corre-sponds with their development of symbolic thought.

In play, we also see many instances of toddlers' growing understanding of cause-and-effect reasoning. They experiment by dropping a ball to watch it roll, then dropping it again from a greater height, then experimenting further to discover what else will roll. A block? A book? A car? Perhaps some peas dropped from a high chair?

Many toddlers excel at imitation. We see our grandchildren imitate familiar actions when they pretend to drive a car or put a baby doll to sleep. As Derek and I read a book about farm animals to our then two-year-old granddaughter Ava, she surprised us— answering our playful "oinks" with her imitation of the very loud grunts of a real pig.

During the toddler years, children make great strides in their ability to communicate. Now they understand more of what others say to them. And, like Ryan, they're better able to commu-nicate what they want and what they'd like to play.

Play also reflects aspects of our grandchildren's social and emotional development. Sometimes we can be so busy with the details of caregiving that it takes a calm moment to appreciate our grandchild's growing abilities. When we take a closer look, we can see toddlers beginning to assert their autonomy and independence while simultaneously becoming more social and eager to become partners in play.

Leni and her granddaughter Luca (21 months) have just returned from a trip to the market. What a hot summer day—a perfect day for water play in the shade of the mulberry tree. Leni takes out an old plastic tub along with three containers for pouring.

But just a minute: Luca has her own ideas for water play. Luca heads to the bathroom for two favorite bath toys, her dog and giraffe. Now she's ready.

They head to the shade of the tree. Leni takes the hose and pours several inches of water into the tub and then adds a little yogurt container. On her own initiative, Luca removes her shoes and socks, sits next to the tub, and plops the dog and giraffe into the water. Picking up the little container and filling it with water, she nods her head thoughtfully and enunciates "wawa" and "mo" as she pours water from the container onto her animals' faces. She gently wipes off some water that's fallen on her dog, murmuring "shhh, shhhh." After a moment she turns around and walks over to the nearby privet bush. Reaching up on her toes, balancing for a moment as she pulls off several tiny green leaves, she drops the leaves in the water next to her dog and giraffe. "Mmmm, mmm," she says and offers them this delicious snack.

Leni's story highlights the inter-related abilities that enable Luca's social, creative, and more complex play. Luca has changed a lot since she was 10 months old and took her first unsteady steps. Her walking is better coordinated and assured. Although she still holds onto Leni for assistance navigating the stairs, she can balance herself well.

Luca's play reflects her emerging ability to use symbols, an ability widely considered the major cognitive development of this age. When toddlers engage in pretend play, they use objects, sounds, and actions to symbolize something else. Pretend play is also called symbolic play. Notice that Luca imitates scenes related to everyday activities like eating, drinking from a bottle—and caring for babies. This shows that she's able to create meaning and express herself through her use of objects (leaves to symbolize food), actions (feeding her dog and giraffe), and communication ("mmmm").

Luca's ability to communicate is also developing rapidly. She recognizes words for a wide range of objects she knows and can follow simple instructions. Leni says that it's become much easier to understand Luca now that she uses short words.

Luca's developing physical, cognitive, and language abilities form the foundations for her social and emotional development, particularly her increasing independence and her eagerness to initiate activities. Leni points out other social and emotional dimensions of Luca's pretend play, such as the way she feeds and comforts her animals. As this story shows, everyday play integrates so many aspects of development.

Keeping Safety First

As grandparents, our role in play expands along with our grandchildren's growing abilities. As babies and toddlers start to creep, crawl, walk, and then run, it becomes more challenging for us to keep up with them—and, more importantly, to keep them safe. Our role in play expands as we constantly monitor the immediate environment, checking for dangers like sharp or small objects or exposed electrical outlets. Safety first is important for us grandparents, too. We're less physically agile than when we were parents, a generation earlier. We need to minimize our risk of falls or other accidents. Now we take greater care that the chair we lean on is stable. We're more attentive to the way we lift our grandchildren and make sure that we clear and unclutter spaces so we can continue with safe, rich play.

Part II. The Glorious Play Years: Three, Four, and Five

So many of the stories grandparents tell are about three, four, and five-year-olds. Why should this be? A host of developmental changes signals the transition from the infant and toddler years to the preschool and kindergarten years.

As our grandchildren develop, we want our relationships to develop as well. We can be as attentive and mindful with older grandchildren as we were when they were infants and toddlers. Now that our grandchildren talk more, we need to become good listeners.

Dr. Rebecca Wheat is an active grandmother of six and a coach at the Principal Leadership Institute. Whether she's speaking with grandparents or educators, she emphasizes the importance of listening. "I think deep listening is so important. It shows appreciation, love, and respect. I think it is particularly important in this age of devices when listening is often not a priority. By listening, we can really learn what they are thinking, and enhance their lead by showing that we respect what they are doing and saying."

From ages three to six, children can do much more than they did before, and their play changes along with their increased abilities. Children and their grandparents enjoy longer and ever more varied and memorable options for play.

Mary's grandchildren live halfway across the country. Because of the COVID-19 pandemic, she cancelled the trip she planned to coincide with the beginning of four-year-old Sophia's preschool. Now Sophia's preschool is open and Mary's more comfortable flying. She has arrived at last! Today, there's an open house for family members. What a perfect opportunity to see this new stage in Sophia's life.

The director tells Mary that Sophia played inside for a while and is now outdoors. Mary sees Sophia with a teacher and several children in an open grassy area with a small mound. Looking around, Mary sees a small climber and slide nearby, and a sand pit with pails and shovels across the yard. There's also a large covered area with a water table and a table with some art materials. What a great place for her to get a better idea of what four-year-olds can do!

How Grandparents Can Support Physical Development Through Play

From ages three through five, children's physical growth and development tend to be more gradual than during infancy. Not visible but essential is the continued development of their brain and nervous system. I'm always astonished to consider that between three and six years the brain grows from about 50 percent to 90 percent of its adult weight.

The continued development of the nervous system enables the faster response times needed for children's better hand-eye coordination and the large muscle movements they need to run and jump. It becomes easier for them to balance and run because their bodies lengthen in proportion to the size of their heads.

Mary watches Sophia and two other children running up, then running or rolling down the mound. Mary notices that Sophia is running more slowly than her friends but faster than when Mary last visited. Running up and down the mound is still challenging for her. Mary knows that Sophia has less strength in her right leg due to a neurological condition that was diagnosed when she was an infant.

When Sophia spots Mary, she rolls down the hill, takes Mary's hand, and tells her with great excitement that she can race around the track two times. She leads Mary to the oval track. Off she goes, calling, "Catch me, Grandma!" Mary takes off after her. Sophia goes fast. Mary realizes that this year she no longer has to pretend to run fast as she did a year ago when she and Sophia played chasing games. Now she really can't keep up!

Sophia's play-centered school is carefully designed for young children ages three through five who have a wide range of developmental abilities and includes children with special needs. Sophia's parents and teachers communicate often to make sure she gets many relaxed and playful opportunities to increase her balance and strength. Mary knows that running is a good exercise for Sophia—and a good exercise for herself as well.

How can you tell how old a child is? If we look at a single child playing in a mixed-age activity at Sophia's school, it's hard to guess that child's age. But when the classes are grouped separately by age, we can tell easily which group is older. Take large muscle strength and development. Four and five-year-old children are more coordinated, agile, and stronger. We see this as we watch them hop, jump, skip, swing, and climb, and see them balancing on scooters and bikes with training wheels. Watching them play chasing games, we notice that they run faster and have greater endurance than three-year-olds do.

THE GIFT OF PLAY

The same is true for fine motor (small muscle) development. Improved hand-eye coordination leads to changes in the way children draw. Many four to five-year-olds can draw people with details like fingers, hair, and shoes. Their increased hand-eye coordination enables them to spin tops, string small beads, and build complicated structures with smaller blocks. Some have developed the coordination needed to write a few letters clearly and enjoy learning to write their own name—and even *your* name, if it's short.

By the time our grandchildren are three years old, our play with them has already changed considerably and continues to change dramatically, greatly expanding the possibilities for playing together. There are so many enticing choices when there's lots of time and space to move around, and so many things to do!

Alan and his three-year-old granddaughter and her friend are playing catch with a large soft ball in the backyard.

Barbara, an avid cyclist, runs after her four-year-old grandson who's learning to ride his bike without training wheels.

Amanda and Beth, two grandmothers, monitor carefully as their three, four, and six-year-old grandchildren climb the rope structures in the park.

Ala, Shasha, and their twin five-year-old grandsons have built a colorful Lego town, and now the boys are busy adding small animals and tiny people.

How Grandparents Can Support Children's Cognitive Development Through Play

Playing with our grandchildren, we observe intriguing changes in their cognitive abilities. Continued changes in the nervous system account for such enhanced aspects of cognitive development as the use of symbols, problem solving, and the ability to plan future actions. We see these abilities manifest in the ways that our grandchildren draw, strategize how to climb the structure at the park, or play games like Simple Simon.

Between ages three and six, grandchildren's ability to use symbols increases exponentially. In their pretend play, three-year-olds tend to use common objects, take familiar roles, and love to play out well-known household routines. At three, our grandson Elijah would say, "It's time to make dinner for my kids. I'm making tacos, tacos with cheddar cheese."

Four and five-year-olds' imaginative play episodes are longer, with themes that reflect their more powerful imagination and their growing sense of a story line. At four, Elijah would make a UPS truck by placing a chair in front of a cardboard carton, then fill the carton with assorted objects for his deliveries. Derek and I could be anywhere in his house and hear him following us, calling out, "OK, sign for your package. Here's your book!"

It's fascinating for us to watch our five-year-old grandchildren learn to coordinate their pretend play with others. One day, for example, we overheard Elijah explaining to his friend Zack, "Hey, if you're gonna be the UPS, you gotta carry the package up to the house."

Symbolic thought is characteristic of a wide range of play from the toddler years throughout adulthood. We see symbolic play when young children play pretend, build with blocks, and paint pictures, when elementary school children tell riddles and play board games, when high school adolescents strategize as they play basketball, when adults do crossword puzzles—and when we play pretend with our grandchildren.

Young children's cognitive development is reflected in their drive to understand their environment, answer questions, and solve problems. They want to understand their social world: "What if Sarah and Harper both ask me to play with them?" "What if we're play-fighting and my teacher tells us to stop fighting, but we're only playing?" or "How do I get picked to play Duck, Duck, Goose?" Children also raise many questions about their physical environment: "How many legs does this spider have?" "How did you blow that bigger bubble?"

> Madison is trying to figure out why the toy car doesn't roll. She turns it over and examines it carefully. She tries to roll the wheels in her hand and then explains to her grandmother, "See ... right here ... see, these front wheels aren't attached right."

If your grandchildren are this age, you might find that sometimes their reasoning seems so competent, while other times their reasoning is difficult to understand. Developmental psychologists point out that such inconsistencies are characteristic of young children's thinking. How can our awareness of this inconsistency influence the way we play with them?

It's helpful to change any assumptions that development is a predictable and steady progression. Instead, we can expect that at one moment, we might be struck by the advances in our grandchild's reasoning as we watch him patiently figure out a puzzle—and understand that moments later, that same grandchild might have difficulty with a simpler puzzle and fling the pieces to the floor.

How Grandparents Can Support Children's Social and Emotional Development Through Play

The sense of connection and joy that children experience in play is closely related to social and emotional development. Emotional development refers to children's capacity to feel a wide range of emotions and to manage or regulate their emotions. In their play, children may respond to major events in their lives such as a new baby and replay fearful situations.

When they were toddlers, we saw our grandchildren developing greater autonomy, wanting to be independent and do things for themselves. A toddler's declaration of "Me do it" becomes the three-year-old's social invitation of "Come, Grandma, wanna play firefighters?"

Play with our grandchildren changes along with their evolving social development. At the same time that they show their autonomy and independence, they're becoming more social. They want to be part of the action, join the play, listen and contribute to conversations, and joke around.

Grandparents know from experience that children's play with their friends and classmates becomes increasingly important from ages three to six. Grandchildren want to have friends, learn how to make friends, and be a friend. They want to learn important social skills, such as learning to enter a group. That's one reason programs for three to five-year-olds are different from programs that care for infants and toddlers. Think about Sophia's preschool and the many opportunities she has to play with a playmate or adult, play in a small group of three or four children, be part of the whole class listening to a story, and, of course, play by herself.

In the following typical example of early parallel play with a friend, in which children play side by side but not together, three-year-old Micah enjoys the company of being near other children in his preschool while not engaging in ongoing social interactions:

> Micah, age three, climbs into the sandbox, looks at Daniel who's piling up sand, and asks, "You're my friend, OK?" Daniel nods silently. Micah moves closer to Daniel and begins digging next to him, each happily making his own pile of sand.

From about age three, children become able to engage in more lengthy and complicated social play. We see their increasing social abilities to play more interactively, keep to a common play theme, and play together for longer times even when conflicts occur.

The child–child conflicts that often arise in play can be important learning moments for children to work out disagreements on their own. They learn through experience that play often stops if they hit or push. When conflicts occur, their anger is more likely to be expressed verbally rather than physically because they want to keep playing with their friends.

From about age four or five we begin to see cooperative play emerge. When we observe closely, we see children's developing ability to take the perspective of others. Our grandchildren are becoming more successful in resolving the conflicts that arise because they understand the other child's point of view. Listening closely, teacher Pat hears, "OK, if you wanna be a princess too, you're gonna need my other wand."

Four-year-olds and especially five-year-olds are becoming ever more independent. They enjoy planning and carrying out increasingly more complex activities to do on their own and socially with others.

At five, Caden and his friend have spent most of the morning creating a fire station out of several crates, blocks, and an old towel. They finished making the hook and ladder fire truck, responded to a fire in a four-story apartment house, and then rushed off to put out a brush fire. As they return to their fire station, Caden calls out, "Grandpa, we're ready to do our fire drill, but first we gotta have our lunches."

Engaging Play Integrates Development

When we look back at the arc of our grandchild's development, we can see that our play changes with the unique flow and timing of our grandchild's development and her or his changing interests. Amparo used to play peekaboo games with Levi and Angel when they were babies. When they were toddlers, they played hide-and-seek. Now these games of younger children have evolved into this boisterous, spirited game of tag.

Levi and Angel are in the park with Amparo on this sunny late afternoon. Levi stares at his shadow—at least five feet long. Amparo walks over to stand next to him. "Wow, Grandma, your shadow is really, really long!" A few minutes later the children are playing shadow tag on the blacktop of the basketball court, trying to catch the other's shadow with their shadow hand. "Let's play tag," Angel shouts. "Who can catch Grandma's shadow?" Amparo runs across the basketball court and over to the playground. She turns, hiding behind the climbing structure as the boys run after her. Next she runs behind a tree, and then finally sprints for the swings. She sits on a swing, her shadow moving in tandem. Angel reaches her first and touches her shadow shoulder. Amparo holds out an arm. Levi, running right behind, lands on the shadow of her hand. "You both got me!" Amparo exclaims.

CHAPTER 4

Play and Language

I remember a trip to a nearby river with friends, grandparents like us. It was sunny and the sky was blue, with fluffy white cumulus clouds drifting by. We saw two grandchildren and their grandmother looking skyward and heard one child shout, "Grandma, look! An elephant on one leg and a ball on a pillow! And that one looks like Gemma's dog Cloudy!" The second child joined in, "That one's a camel with a baby camel," then paused and continued more quietly, "Look … the shadows of the clouds are moving on the water." When their grandmother saw we were looking their way, she smiled, sharing her delight.

Play and language form a natural partnership. Whenever play is mutual and joyful, play and communication are inseparable. Everyday playful experiences—relaxed times when children feel no pressure to "learn"—are perfect for enhancing their abilities to understand others and be understood.

Listen to grandparents and you'll hear us celebrating developmental milestones in our grandchildren's communication, from their coos and smiles, to their first words, to their imaginative stories. We're acutely aware of how quickly children change, and we want to savor each moment. In this chapter, we'll consider how children communicate, look at ways of appreciating what our grandchildren do and what we do together, and see ways to expand our repertoire.

With all the articles and books available on children's language development, why focus on children's play? Families often ask this question when they think of all the commercial toys and programs that promise to "promote your child's language." Upon investigation, however, we find most of these programs are routine lesson-type activities that don't relate to our grandchild's interests, strengths, needs, and creative abilities.

Educators and developmental scientists emphasize that young children don't need costly commercial toys or programs. Children's everyday playful interactions support their language learning. Especially important for young children are times for social play with their peers and caring adults—like grandparents!

Looking at Play Through the Lens of Communication

Communications with our grandchildren are playful when our purpose is mutual pleasure rather than a learning goal like learning the alphabet. Some communication is wordless, as when four-month-old Walker expresses his delight by smiling back at his older brother and his grandmother as they sit on the floor beside him.

Or think about the nonverbal communication taking place when five-year-old Amalie appears in the living room, her face decorated with stripes of orange and purple face paint. She looks up at her grandmother Grace, who responds by quizzically raising her eyebrows. Then they both laugh.

Some communication consists of lengthy verbal exchanges that pick up where they left off the previous week. Four-year-old Aaron runs to greet Grandpa Steve at the front door with cheery greetings of "Humpty Dumpty frumty, mumty!" and "Baba black sheep, meep, bo beep!" Aaron is recalling the fun of his grandpa's last visit when they made old rhymes into silly new ones.

Particular times and places seem to inspire playful conversations. Think of family parties and playgrounds—busy times and places when we're with lots of people having a good time. We probably feel more playful just being around other people with playful dispositions.

Maybe these conversations occur more often when we're relaxed and calmly enjoying the beauty of nature with our grandchildren. Or perhaps these places evoke our abilities to communicate joyfully, mutually, and playfully.

Whenever you're playing, your communication is playful as well. You and your grandchild might be outdoors blowing bubbles or inside building with blocks or drawing and coloring. Perhaps your grandchildren involve you in their pretend play or ask that you read them a story. Even when you're involved in routines like washing dishes or changing diapers, playfulness can change your mood and delight your grandchildren.

Connecting Generations Through Language

Through play we have an opportunity to share our family heritage, our cultural heritage, and our human heritage. When we think about how language connects generations, it's not simply the particular language we speak but also how we use language that forges connections. Grandchildren often love hearing stories about when their parents were children and listening to how we played when we were kids.

Do you enjoy telling stories, playing games from your childhood, or singing songs? What do you recall about how you played with adults when you were a child? How did you play with your own child?

Before computers and television, and in the distant past before books, cultures around the world were oral. Cultural customs, beliefs, and history were passed down from one generation to the next through rituals, conversations, sayings, songs, and stories. In our own lifetime we've witnessed language evolving. Today, some families retain their oral heritage, while others do not. Nonetheless, we draw from oral traditions when we sing folk songs, tell folktales, use proverbs, or share favorite stories and sayings passed down to us from our own parents and grandparents.

Oral traditions are retained in the ways we play with young children. Think of all the lullabies and songs, and tickling, clapping, and rocking games, and the stories for infants and young children that we pass down from one generation to the next. By celebrating these traditions, we're connecting generations—giving our grandchild a gift of play that was our own inheritance.

Listen to grandparents from any country playing with infants and toddlers. You'll hear similarities in the way we speak and in our games, songs, and stories. We use language that appeals to young children because the words are simple and the sentences are short. Traditional games, songs, and stories feature catchy rhythms, repetitions, and rhymes. And all around the world, young grandchildren are enthusiastic audiences and eager to join in.

What games, stories, and playful songs do you remember from your childhood? Have you shared these with your grandchildren? What new ones have you learned from watching your son or daughter play with your grandchild? Whether or not it's our conscious intention, when we play with our grandchildren, we celebrate traditions we love and we also create new ones.

Some games and playful songs derive from family traditions we've learned from our own grandparents, parents, or siblings. Others we enjoy even though we don't remember where we learned them. Some songs we sang with our own children are now part of the broader culture—like the Beatles' song "Yellow Submarine."

As I write this, I think about several games I've played with my grandchildren and wonder if they'll remember any of them when they're older. Sometimes a grandchild will remind us of a song we used to sing: "Do you remember? When I was little, we'd dance and you'd sing 'She'll Be Coming 'Round the Mountain' in a funny voice." We create these gifts of play together. Some traditions are passed from grandparent to grandchild. Others are created and passed on from grandchild to grandparent.

Sharing Stories: Playful Storytelling

Whatever our age, we can turn to oral storytelling traditions to enrich our lives. I used to think of storytelling as a special talent for inventing and spinning a tale, a talent only some people had (I wasn't one of them). Now that I've read more about storytelling and the call of stories, I realize there are so many different kinds of stories and so many ways to tell these stories. While I don't think I'm good at spinning tales, I do enjoy telling stories.

Stories inform, entertain, and intrigue us, and show us a universe of possibilities, real and imagined. Some stories are embedded in poems, songs, legends, and folktales. Others are factual accounts of adventures in nature, about animals, plants, and the planet.

Telling stories and hearing stories deepens our relationships with family and friends. Stories connect us with other people, times, and places. Whether we're grandchildren or grand-parents, storytelling helps us understand one another's emotions, thoughts, and experiences. We recall wonderful stories that spring from our imagination as well as stories about our experiences. As grandparents, we know that this begins quite early:

Vincente (22 months) and his grandfather are outdoors, delighting in blowing bubbles. Today's memorable achievement: instead of inhaling the bubble solution, Vincente blows out and actually makes a bubble. He and his grandfather watch as Vincente's very first bubble floats away.

They go back inside and Vincente looks for his dad while excitedly repeating, "bubba ... bubba ... bubba ..."

Then he reaches his arms out toward his grandfather, repeating "bubba, bubba!" and follows this with lengthy babbling phrases. He shares his story with great intensity and dramatic inflections, followed by a look of satisfaction.

This is an exciting moment for Vincente's dad and grandfather, particularly because his pediatrician raised concerns that, although Vincente comprehends some phrases, his speech may be delayed.

The next story shows that virtual visits can be rich moments for playful storytelling. Notice how Silas subtly invites his three-year-old grandson Cameron to continue making up the story. And, although grandfather and grandson are video chatting, their conversation flows seamlessly.

> Silas begins: "Once upon a time, there was a little squirrel named Sammy and he wanted to play. Sammy the squirrel was at the park when he saw Cameron. 'Cameron,' Sammy said, 'Do you like to play? I want to play with you.' And Cameron said, 'Yes, let's play. Let's play pretend.' So Sammy the squirrel and Cameron played pretend. What do you think they did?"
>
> Silas pauses and waits, and then Cameron continues: "Me and Sammy the squirrel played in the park. I chased Sammy. Then Sammy chased me. Then I caughted him. Then we ate ice cream called rocky road ice cream, my favorite kind, and Sammy the squirrel likes it too."

Young children delight in the straightforward narratives and repetition found in picture books and songs. One grandmother told me she used a simple story line with lots of repetition to emphasize how eager she was to visit her grandchild:

> "I'm so glad to be at your house and play with you! This morning, I got up and thought, 'Today's the day I play with Mila.' But first I had to eat breakfast. So I ate my breakfast. While I ate breakfast, I thought, 'Today's the day I play with Mila.'

"But then, I had to get dressed and brush my teeth and brush my hair. And guess what I was thinking as I got dressed and brushed my teeth and brushed my hair? I was thinking," Grandma says with emphasis, "'Today's the day I play with Mila.'"

"Next, I had to get on the bus and ride to your house. So I went down the stairs, and out the door, walked to the bus stop, waited for the bus, then got on the bus, and sat down near the bus driver.

"The bus driver asked me, 'Where are you going today?' And I said, 'I'm going to Mila's house because ... Today's the day I play with my granddaughter Mila!' Then the bus driver said, 'What a lucky grandmother you are!' And I said, 'Yes, I'm soooo lucky!'

"When we got to the bus stop near your house, I got off the bus and I walked around the corner to Edith Street where your house is. I walked to the green house with the numbers 4835 near the front door and I rang the bell.

"Then you and your daddy came to the door. And then you both gave me great big, wonderful hugs, and I gave you and your daddy great big wonderful hugs, too. And all the while I was still thinking ..."

Grandma pauses, raises her eyebrows, and looks at Mila and her dad. Then they all say together: "Today's the day I play with Mila!"

Tips for Engaging Storytelling

Here are some tips to engage your young listeners, whether you're making up your own story, telling a story about something that really happened, retelling a traditional tale, or reading a story from a book.

➤ Think about a good opening. "Once upon a time" is a classic for an imaginary tale. "Did I ever tell you about the time ...?" can be a good opening for real experiences. Relating the story to your grandchild's life is almost certain to engage interest.

➤ Keep the story simple.

➤ Use vivid language to enthrall your grandchild.

➤ Reflect your own pleasure and create the mood using tone, emphasis, dramatic pauses, and movement.

➤ Use repetition and relevant questions to invite your grandchild's engagement and active participation.

➤ Plan how to make the ending more memorable by relating the story once again to your grandchild's experiences, by summing up, or by ending with a repeated phrase that your grandchild can anticipate and say with you.

Play and Language Development

Picture these three scenes of grandparents observing communication, language, and literacy "in action" during play:

It's after lunch, almost naptime. Jake, 13 months old at this time, has been busy all morning, accompanying his actions with babbling. Right now he's found his stuffed dog and his board book, *Where Is Spot?* "Jake, do you want to read your book?" I ask. He carries the dog and the book to the couch where I'm sitting, then holds his arms up to tell me that he wants to sit with me. *Where Is Spot?* is a favorite book because the language is very repetitive, and Jake loves the "peekaboo" pages with the flaps he can open to reveal a hidden animal.

Zoë, three years old at this time and just starting preschool, often engages her family members, friends, dolls, and stuffed animals in long episodes of imaginative, pretend play. This morning she carries an armful of animals and her toy phone and announces, "We're going to my school's circle time." She stops suddenly and sighs dramatically, "Another call. I'm busy now." She puts her animals down on the rug, puts the phone to her ear, and declares, "If you want to say something to Zoë, please leave her a message."

Reuben, five years old, asks his Grandpa Enrique, "Did you ever see *Mary Poppins*?" Enrique responds, "Yes, I saw the movie a long time ago with your mom when she was a kid. Can you remind me about the story?" Reuben leans forward and gestures dramatically, indicating that he's ready to begin. "You're gonna like this story ... Mary Poppins is magic. She goes to live with Jane and Michael in their house. Their dad doesn't want her there. They like her because she's magic. She makes medicine taste like candy. She has a friend Bert. He dances on the roof. They go to an upside-down party and float on the ceiling and eat lots of birthday cake. Then they go back home and their dad is glad Mary Poppins is there. But she has to go away. Then they all get sad."

Grandparents know that even young infants use nonverbal expressions and movements to communicate feelings and thoughts. The story about 13-month-old Jake illustrates that, well before infants and toddlers speak their first sentences, they begin to understand the languages spoken around them. This ability to understand information depends on what educational psychologists call *receptive language*.

The ability to communicate depends on what linguists call *expressive language*. Think about the words three-year-old Zoë used: "If you want to say something to Zoë, please leave her a message." This sentence shows that she knows how to order the words so we easily understand her. Throughout childhood and across the lifespan, people's capacity to understand language is greater than their ability to speak.

Of course, the timing and rate at which individual children become able to communicate vary considerably. When older infants and toddlers babble, they're imitating the rhythm, tone, and sounds of the language or languages they hear. Many infants utter their first words at about one year and, by about two years, they use sentences of two or three words.

Between three and six years, children's expressive language develops rapidly as they learn the vocabulary and the sentence structures they need to communicate their ideas, desires, and experiences. Linguists estimate that by the time they are six years old, most children know between 8,000 and 16,000 words.

When children like Zoë and her brother Elijah learn two languages, they're learning not only to understand what is being said but also, importantly, to express their thoughts and feelings by means of vocabulary and grammar that may be quite different from one language to another. For example, when Elijah was two, he would speak to me in English and then, turning to his father, switch to Dutch. Grandparents with bilingual grandchildren are often amazed that their three or four-year-old grandchild knows which languages a relative or friend speaks—and which they don't understand.

Grandparents are intrigued by words invented by their grandchildren. When my granddaughter Ava was four, she greeted me with her exciting news: "I saw such a scary movie, *Winnie the Pooh*. It was so freakout-ish." A friend told a story about taking care of her two-and-a-half-year-old grandnephew who loves cars and trucks. He was looking out the window and watching neighborhood children skate. He'd never seen skates before and was intrigued that skates have wheels. Excitedly, he pointed and exclaimed, "Shoe-trucks!"

Based on our experience, we grandparents know that our grandchildren's language acquisition is complicated. This achievement is even more remarkable when we appreciate how much their language develops during the first years of life. Indeed, language development is one of the hottest topics of research in early childhood development.

To better appreciate this achievement and the mysteries of language development, take a closer look at the stories in this chapter. They raise some of the questions that make language acquisition a primary focus of study for psychologists, linguists, and educators.

For example, how has Jake figured out what a particular word refers to—in this case, the word *book*? And when three-year-old Zoë declares, "If you want to say something to Zoë, please leave her a message," how has she figured out this basic structure of English grammar?

The mystery deepens when we consider that most people in the world know two or more languages. How do children learn the structures and vocabulary for different languages? I wonder about this when I hear Zoë saying the same thing in Dutch: *"Laat een berichtje achter op deze telefoon als je iets tegen Zoë wil zeggen."* ("If you want to say something to Zoë, please leave her a message on her phone.")

I spoke with my friend and colleague Dr. Linda Kroll to learn more about language acquisition and hear stories about her own grandchildren's language development. A professor at Mills College for many years, Linda taught early childhood education courses on language acquisition, cognitive development, and reading. After retiring last year, she and her husband have spent many afternoons taking care of their two grandchildren aged two and five.

Linda emphasizes that young children have to figure out grammatical constructions themselves and that they don't "get it" if we just correct them. For example, a preschooler might say, "I goed to the store." The grandparent then corrects, "I went to the store." To which the preschooler says, "Yes, I goed to the store."

Consider this story that illustrates how young children experiment with grammar as they try to figure out basic grammatical structures. Linda's grandson is fascinated with numbers. At two and a half, he can count by rote to 20 even though he doesn't fully comprehend what the numbers mean. Recently he asked her, "What comes after seven?" Linda asked what he thought, and he replied "eight." She nodded and added, "Eight comes after seven." As he wandered into the living room, she heard him repeating that sentence structure and substituting the numbers in sequence: "Eight comes after seven. Eight comes after seven." Then, "Nine comes after eight. Ten comes after nine."

Linda also explained that young children spend a great deal of time practicing communication conventions. A good example is "turn-taking." She points out that when infants are young, we model turn-taking when we take both sides of the conversation, for example, "Do you want to get up? ... Yes, you do." Linda told of listening to her granddaughter, a kindergartner, play with her dolls. The dolls were having an engaging conversation, taking turns to speak and thoughtfully responding to each other. You might hear your own grandchild practice turn-taking when you hear him talking with his stuffed animal: "Here's food." "Yum." "More?" "Yum."

Playful Books and Imagination

Next time you're in a library or bookstore, check out the children's section and you'll probably see someone else who looks like a grandparent. When you think about young children and language, you might think of curling up on a comfortable couch with your grandchild and a favorite picture book. It's wonderful when this happens in person, but there are ways to create these special moments when personal visits are not possible. Whether we're sitting next to our grandchildren or seeing them at a distance, the pleasure of reading aloud makes these special times.

I recently saw a baby T-shirt that read "So Many Books. So Little Time." Today tens of thousands more books for young children are available than when we were young. These include books of nonfiction and fiction, poetry, information, and fantasy. Happily, we also have a growing number of books about the diversity of families, families in our communities as well as those living far away. More children's books than ever before are available in different languages, so families enjoy books with their children in their native language. The small library near my home has children's books written in Spanish, Chinese, Japanese, and Russian, as well as those translated into English from other languages.

With so many options, how do you choose?

Start by thinking of the picture books you loved hearing when you were a child or enjoyed reading to your own children. Some are now classics and still available. Many grandchildren love to hear our introduction, "I used to read this book to your daddy when he was your age."

Over the years, children's librarians have helped me discover books that have become our favorites. Your local children's librarian not only knows what books many young children love hearing but can also help you select books of special interest for your own grandchild.

Libraries, bookstores, and online resources also have lists of recommended books for infants, toddlers, preschoolers, and kindergartners. I recommend lists compiled by expert, noncommercial sources like the American Library Association and the National Association for the Education of Young Children. (See the Resources list at the end of this book for links to these reading lists.)

What makes a good picture book? First of all, no matter who recommends the book, the most important question is will you and your grandchild find the story and illustrations appealing and interesting? It's important to browse and leisurely preview books when you're on your own without a small child.

Below are some questions and tips to help guide your selections. With so many books to choose from, if you find yourself answering "no" to any of these questions, I suggest you look for a different book.

1. Quickly page through the book to get a sense of the story and the illustrations. Does the book immediately appeal to you? Is it one you think your grandchild will understand and enjoy?

2. Read the text thoroughly and slowly as if you were reading it aloud. Notice the author's choice of words and the rhythm of the sentences. Does this book lend itself to reading aloud? More importantly, will you enjoy reading it aloud to your grandchild?

3. Remember that evocative illustrations as well as text are key to a good picture book. Are the illustrations appealing? Do the text and illustrations go together to tell the story and create the mood? Do you find the text and illustrations playful, imaginative, creative, or humorous? Carefully review both the text and illustrations to make sure both are free from ethnic, racial, or gender stereotyping.

4. Consider whether the text and illustrations might be too detailed and complicated for your grandchild. This is especially important if you plan to read the book during a virtual visit. If so, look for a book with text and illustrations that can be seen clearly at a distance.

See the Resources list at the end of this book for lists of excellent young children's books, and ask your local librarian for lists of recommendations. Look for books that are playful, imaginative, and sometimes laugh-out-loud funny. Some are written by well-loved authors. Others have won recent awards for children's literature.

I think we enjoy our reading more when we're aware that our purpose is not to finish the story but simply to have fun together. Sometimes you'll finish the book, sometimes you won't. Many grandparents find that when a book is a success, their grandchild may ask them to read and then reread the book several times in a row.

On some days, though, one of you will decide that this book isn't the right one for that day and opt to choose another one. On other days, the story and illustrations are perfect, inspiring playful imaginings, discussions, and activities. Playfulness and creativity are important. Instead of considering these playful wanderings as interruptions to storytelling, you might pause and bookmark where you are. Then, you might see where your grandchild's conversation leads to and plan to return to the book later or even another day.

Tips for Playful Reading

➤ To promote focus and avoid the wiggles, make sure that everyone is sitting comfortably.

➤ Position the pictures and text at a height and distance where all grandchildren have a clear view. Make sure that the light is good so everyone can appreciate the colors and details in the illustrations. For virtual visits, grandparents can read and talk about a book while a parent or older sibling positions the book so the grandparent can read easily.

➤ Read in a relaxed way so that your voice conveys your interest and enjoyment. Picture books are like poems. They have relatively few words, which authors chose very carefully to create the story line and tone. In good picture books, the illustrations play an equally important part in telling the story and enhancing the tone.

(cont.)

Tips for Playful Reading (cont.)

➢ Remember that books are objects that infants and toddlers want to explore, mouth, and touch. Decide with older children which books they will share.

➢ With older toddlers, preschoolers, and kindergartners, take ample time to relate the story to your grandchild's experiences. Remember that children's ability to understand language is much greater than their ability to speak. Answer your grandchild's questions, but consider keeping explanations brief if you decide not to interrupt the flow of the story.

➢ Remember that older preschoolers and kindergartners enjoy relating the story and illustrations to the growing trove of personal experiences they like to share with you.

➢ Good readers—and future readers—learn to actively anticipate the story line. You might ask preschoolers and kindergartners a question or simply "wonder" what will happen on the next page. It's fun to encourage them to think about the story line by asking you to do the same thing. "Grandpa, what do you think will happen next?"

➢ Appreciate picture books as springboards for your own and your grandchild's imaginative storytelling.

THE GIFT OF PLAY

Because we recognize the importance of cultivating a love of books, grandparents raise concerns about times when a grandchild doesn't seem interested. It's important and reassuring not to be discouraged by such indifference. Even young children already differ in their interests, fascinated by one book and disinterested in another. We have to think about a good match for the individual grandchild and consider the story and illustrations as well as the tone of a book.

Grandparents have asked me why some children listen for only a moment before running off to a new activity while others ask you to read the same book over and over again. Keep in mind that children's development is rarely linear. An infant who loves to hear books may grow into a preschooler who's rarely interested and, of course, vice versa.

These early behaviors don't predict how much joy grandchildren will have as adult readers. And as long as we're playful and patient and frequently tell stories and read books with our grandchildren, they'll remember the joy of hearing and sharing books with their grandparents.

Extending Your Grandchildren's Early Efforts as Storytellers, Illustrators, and Authors

Emergent literacy refers to young children's development of the attitudes and abilities that lead to literacy. Most obviously, this includes children listening to stories being told, listening to books being read, and retelling stories to you. It also includes drawing "real" pictures about their lives ("this is me") and imaginary or fantasy pictures ("this is a monster"). Many children love homemade books they can keep and look at day after day.

Once I became a grandparent, I started observing other grandparents more closely. I have noticed we do many things early childhood experts recommend to support emergent literacy.

There are many playful ways to foster the natural process of emergent literacy. When your young grandchild begins to show spontaneous interest in writing or reading, good advice is to avoid "teaching as you were taught," like teaching phonics rules. Playful interactions promote young children's futures as speakers, readers, and writers.

Emergent literacy develops early as toddlers and preschoolers learn to turn the pages of a book as we read to them. Everyday experiences like looking at street signs, going to the store, and, of course, talking about the books we read help build literacy. Sometimes toddlers and preschoolers will sit down by themselves with a favorite book and page through it, "reading" to themselves as they've seen you read to them.

Older preschoolers, kindergartners, and first graders can often recall the main characters in a story and may be able to relate the sequence of the main events. Without formal instruction, some older preschoolers and kindergartners recognize familiar words in their environment such as "STOP" and "pizza," and learn to read the names of family members. Experiences like these tend to stimulate the connection between hearing stories and compre-hending written language.

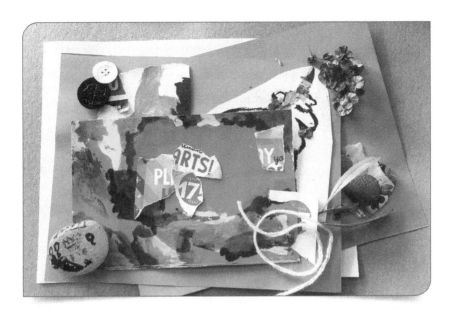

You and your grandchild might have fun creating a family photo book with captions your grandchild dictates to you. On another day, you might make a collage from food labels that have letters or label the artistic creation your grandchild has made.

For example, last spring when my grandniece Luca was sick, my sister Leni gave her some clay to play with. Luca created a small squishy blob she named a "cold germ." After it dried, Luca painted it and asked her grandmother to write a sign to tell everyone what it was. Since then, Luca's creation captures everyone's attention as it sits on her grandparents' bookshelf along with the sign: "Luca's Cold Germ."

Some grandchildren enjoy making up, dictating, and illustrating stories. Younger ones might dictate a short, one-sentence story that you can write on the top of the page, leaving the space on the bottom for their illustrations. Older preschoolers and kindergartners often enjoy making little books with stories they dictate and illustrate.

Keep in mind that emergent literacy includes the child's experiences of being carefully listened to as well. We grandparents are wonderful listeners when we're attentive to a toddler babbling as she arranges her puppets, when we ponder a question a preschooler asks, or when we sit patiently as a kindergartner recounts the events of his school day.

When we're good listeners, our grandchildren know we're interested in what they have to say. Over time, they're likely to develop a sense of themselves as engaging storytellers, illustrators, and authors.

CHAPTER 5

Pretend Play

Pretend play offers a portal for grandparents to enter into the universe of their grandchild's imagination. Three-year-old Jake explains what it means to pretend:

"It's when you are, but you're not."

Pretend play intrigues us. So many stories we tell about our grandchildren are about pretend play. A toddler wearing his firefighter's hat and racing his little firetruck along the edge of the carpet. Another cradling his stuffed doggie and whispering softly as he puts his "baby" to sleep. A preschooler inviting her grandfather to take care of her babies and announcing, "You be the daddy. I'm going to the store for more milk." Later that afternoon, she dons her flowing cape and charges across the yard, alerting her grandparents to danger, "The monsters are coming!" A kindergartner instructs his younger brother: "Now we're playing restaurant. I'll write the orders and you cook the kebabs tonight."

Pretend play is also called make-believe play, fantasy play, and dramatic play. Younger children often play by themselves, telling themselves the story and sometimes speaking aloud. When older children play with others, they create an evolving story line that can become quite complicated.

Grandparents see these creative flights of imagination happening everywhere. Their stories tell of the myriad dimensions of pretend play and the ways that they encourage and participate. My friend Ann in Australia sent this story:

When Minka was four, she was really into fantasy play—fairies in particular. When Ann visited, she was immediately drawn into the latest fairy adventure. This time, Minka and the fairies had set up a coffee shop (which also sold hot chocolate and muffins) under a tree, hidden by bushes. But the trouble was, when it rained, they all got wet.

So Minka and Ann set about building a cubby house— cubbies in Australia are usually outside and made of sticks. Together they worked out how long the sticks would need to be to reach across the tree branches and make the roof ("a bit over Gran's head"), and how they could intertwine smaller sticks with the bushes to make the walls.

They scrambled all over the place finding the right materials, and then got happily sweaty and dirty putting it all together. Next they cleared away the leaves on the ground, found some logs and rocks to sit on, rolled them into place, and found some moss for the carpet.

Then it was time to invite Minka's parents, Alex and Emma, and baby brother Harlow to afternoon tea. First, Minka asked Alex for help placing the last of the roof sticks, which were too high up for her and Ann. Afterward, Minka carried her tea set into the cubby after stopping at the nearby water faucet to fill the creamer with "milk." Then they all squashed into the cubby, Harlow on his dad's lap.

With a practiced air, Minka served cappuccino in the gumnuts (eucalyptus acorns) to the grown-ups, and she helped the fairies make hot chocolate—"No, Flossy, you have to heat the milk first." "This is the chocolate" (offering some little seeds to her invisible friends). "Don't make it too hot for Harlow."

(cont.)

(cont.)

Alex and Emma admired the coffee shop cubby, congratulated Minka on the fine coffee, asked for "seconds" of the muffins, and asked Minka to tell them the names of her fairy friends and where they lived. Harlow looked slightly bemused but happily "drank" his invisible chocolate. Minka told her Gran that the fairies were really glad to have a proper coffee shop, but next time the grown-ups came, they'd have to pay for their drinks.

The next time Ann visited, the cubby was worse for wear, so they started all over again under another tree—this time making a school room.

Notice how Minka moves flexibly between what is real and pretend, ordinary and fantastic, and physically possible and impossible. Magical fairy creatures play familiar roles. Despite this fantasy element, her underlying theme is one we see often in young children's play—feeding and taking care of others. Minka's fantasy takes place in a café, a setting that's familiar to Minka. One reason I find this story so appealing is the way Minka reverses the roles. Here it is Minka and her fairy friends who feed and take care of the others who, in real life, take care of her.

Minka is aware of herself both as a character in the play and as Minka herself. She transforms herself from being Minka to being one fairy, then another, and back to Minka. She effort-lessly moves back and forth between real and pretend characters (the fairies), and interacts with the "real people," her parents, her brother, and her gran.

Minka's miniature tea set is a prop that "cues" for scenes like this. (If, instead, Minka had chosen miniature toy lions and bears, she'd probably have invited her family to a circus instead of a tea party.) Minka improvises a familiar "script," going to a café for coffee, hot chocolate, and muffins.

It's no wonder that people who research children's dramatic play use theater terms like *roles*, *scripts*, and *improvisation* to describe how children, like actors in a play, are aware of themselves moving in and out of their pretend play. And as in theater productions, there's a need for different roles. Minka is writer, producer, and director—and of course a child who is thrilled when she gets glowing "reviews" from her parents!

Notice that Minka's pretend play has a quality found in all pretense—the use of symbols. In pretend play, the child pretends that one object stands for another. Minka uses the little seeds to stand for chocolate and water to stand for coffee or hot chocolate.

Pretend play gives children free rein to imagine and create. And children's imaginations capture our imagination, too. Grandparents might be surprised reading about the multiple aspects of Minka's pretend play, her thoughtful imagination, creativity, social skills, and language. She and her gran needed physical strength and coordination to build the cubby. Pretend play also supports children's dispositions, such as perseverance and engagement, that grandparents want to encourage.

Pretend play can seem so simple yet is so multifaceted. No wonder grandparents are so enthralled, and so are early childhood teachers and researchers.

Jerome and Dorothy Singer were researchers and authors of numerous books on young children's play. They found that pretend play provides children with a wide range of experiences that foster their curiosity and drive to explore alternative strategies. Of special interest to grandparents is their finding that children who often engage in make-believe play are more likely to be happier and more flexible when they come across new situations.

Vivian Paley's books also champion make-believe play and provide interested grandparents with an in-depth understanding of the central role of fantasy play in development, including how play fosters imagination, creativity, and flexibility. Paley was a passionate advocate for keeping dramatic play at the heart of young children's schooling. For more than 30 years as a kinder-garten teacher, she kept daily observations of children's dramatic play. Several of her books have special appeal to grandparents. Over the years, I've recommended them to grandparents and parents as delightful bedtime reading. For example, in *Mollie Is Three* and *The Boy Who Would Be a Helicopter*, Paley follows a single child's dramatic play throughout the year with the same interest and care as grandparents fascinated by their grandchild's play.

In her books, Paley explains that playing together helps young children connect more deeply with others as they create a joint story line over time. *Bad Guys Don't Have Birthdays* follows her kindergarten class through a year in which the children dealt with the themes of good/bad and danger/rescue.

Do you remember *Little Red Riding Hood*? For several children in Paley's classroom, this story became the topic of pretend play over multiple weeks as they created versions with complicated twists and turns (Paley, 2004, pp. 20–21). This is the way it began:

"Pretend you're reading Red Riding Hood." Jilly says, handing me the book.

"Not really reading?"

"No, pretend you're reading and I'm really pretending." Later, in the doll corner, Jilly explains herself further.

"You be the mother," she tells Cora. "You'll have to come with me in case there's a wolf."

"First we see the hunter," Cora decides. "He's already banged at the wolf!"

"No, see, this is the first real way it goes. The wolf sees the mother and so he runs away."

The Development of Pretend Play

Grandparents are fascinated by their grandchildren's fantasy play. We watch as our grandchildren creatively frame the plot, establish the setting, and create the characters and themes. Over time, we can see how the themes reflect their development.

In *Play at the Center of the Curriculum*, my co-authors and I discuss why different themes come to the fore at different ages (Van Hoorn, Nourot, Scales, & Alward, 2015). Toddlers and young preschoolers are trying to cope with frequent separations, like parents leaving for work. They also know that parents and other adults are bigger, powerful, and able to do more. And they're the people who make the rules.

When we watch children's play carefully, we sometimes see these issues reflected in the themes of their pretend play. Pretend play themes for toddlers and young preschoolers involve opposites such as separation/reunion, small/big, being lost/found, good/bad, forbidden/permissible. Have you seen any of these themes in your grandchild's pretend play?

When children are three, four, and five years old, earlier themes persist while new ones emerge that reflect their growing development. Now we see themes such as love/hate, danger/rescue, life/death. In fact, we grandparents sometimes see children play out scenes of life and death on a grand scale. Have you ever seen a child pretend to die dramatically, then "get alive" and happily run off to play some more?

Indeed, I think that one reason pretend play fascinates us grandparents is that it reminds us of our own childhood memories that still echo with magic. Pretend play also captivates our adult interest in drama—and specifically in themes that are the stuff of ancient legends and myths, Shakespeare's plays, and *Star Wars*. Themes such as love/hate, good/bad, separation/reunion, danger/rescue, permissible/forbidden, and death/rebirth resonate with us because they are powerful, existential themes.

Complex dramatic play develops throughout the early years. As grandparents, we are delighted when toddlers first begin to engage in pretend play. From about 18 to 30 months, toddlers usually play by themselves, although they take a step toward social play when they offer their grandparents the "yummy soup" they've just made.

In pretend play, younger children tend to use familiar household objects and enjoy playing with dolls, toy cars and trucks, miniature people, and stuffed animals that resemble what they're meant to symbolize. They play out everyday family scenes of how adults take care of children as they feed their stuffed animals or croon their dolls to sleep.

Although grandparents who live at a distance enjoy viewing pretend play virtually, it can be difficult to participate. Sometimes, it's actually easier to engage online at this age than when grand-children are older. For example, grandparents can hold up a puppet or doll for two and three-year-old children who are pretend play novices—sometimes, I've simply held up my hand covered in a sock and had memorable conversations with stuffed owls, pig puppets, and even blue toy trucks.

If we watch carefully, we can sometimes learn about our grandchild's needs and fears. For example, many toddlers have difficulty controlling their impulse to bite others when they are angry. We might see a toddler gently give a bottle to a crocodile puppet one moment and, in the next, sternly repeat the oft-heard warning, "Stop biting!"

Sometimes toddlers replay exciting events, like eating cupcakes at a birthday party. At other times, they try to understand situations in which they got hurt or felt scared. For example, Miles is talking to himself as he sits near his grandparents: "I better be careful. I fall off and I fall in the water, and here's where the water ends and Grandma and Grandpa and Mama and Dad come."

Children's imaginations soar as they grow older. When children are about three or four, their dramatic play becomes more sophisticated. At this age, they can use any object to stand for whatever they need for their pretend play. A block becomes a phone. Pebbles become money. And, as Minka's story shows, a gumnut is a perfect cup for cappuccino. At this age, we're sometimes astonished to watch our grandchildren's quick transformations from one character to another.

When she was three, Ava visited the fire station with Nana Holly, her beloved "local grandmother." Firefighter Scott gave them a grand tour, showing Ava the long hoses and lifting her on to the driver's seat of the hook and ladder fire truck. The next morning, when Derek and I arrived, we found Ava gussied up in her firefighter's outfit and playing with her fire truck. But wait—she remembered her Baby Dawn and picked her up to nurse. A few moments later, still dressed as a firefighter, she went over to her basket of stuffed animals and pulled out her puppy. She placed it next to Baby Dawn and announced she was going to find birthday candles for their party.

I wondered what inspired her to choose these roles and transformations. Her choice of firefighter seems obvious, and her transformation to nursing mom understandable, but what about the break in action to get her stuffed puppy? Had she heard a dog barking on the street? And what train of thought led to the birthday party scene? When a preschooler becomes a firefighter then a nursing mom, then has a birthday party, she learns to take perspectives of others as she tries to communicate "this is a firefighter—this is a puppy" so we can figure out what she's doing.

It can be difficult for children with developmental delays who can become frustrated when it takes them longer than their peers to understand another's perspective. How does a child feel if she's pretending to be a ferocious tiger, but we don't understand and gently pat her head? I have often seen a child's grandparents give the child the support they need, for example, by observing closely to understand the child's intent, then following the child's lead: "Now I know you're a very big scary tiger!"

At three, four, and five, children are learning to understand the perspective of others. When my grandson Elijah was three, he liked to play "making dinner." I have a vivid memory of Elijah as he prepped the food and declared, "It's time to make dinner for my kids. I'm making tacos, tacos with cheddar cheese."

I remember this scene as a new milestone for him. He was considering his actions from my perspective. He had stepped out of his role as "a parent making dinner" to make sure I'd under-stand what he was doing. We are well aware that understanding the perspective of others is important for our grandchildren, not only during their childhood but also throughout their lives as adults.

Young children are also learning how to behave in different social situations. "This is how I should behave in a restaurant" or "Here's what kids do at a birthday party." We often see them include these understandings when they have make-believe birthday parties or pick out favorite foods at pretend restaurants. Bilingual children learn not only when to switch languages but also how to handle differences in cultures, for example, how to greet Tia Linda from Mexico and Tante Janneka from the Netherlands.

At this age it's common for us grandparents to see our grandchild playing with an imaginary companion, which can provide support for trying new things. Patricia Nourot, one of the co-authors of our book *Play at the Center of the Curriculum*, loved to tell the story of sitting in a neighborhood restaurant next to a family with a daughter who looked about five. At one point, the mother told the daughter that she was old enough to go to the restroom by herself. The daughter got up, hesitated, and then went back to her chair, where she reached out to take the hand of her imaginary companion and the pair strode confidently to the restroom.

As children's social and cognitive capabilities grow, grandparents may enjoy watching them playing with siblings and friends. Many grandparents like being casual audience members, curious to watch the plot develop and notice which child plays which role.

Early social dramatic play usually involves small groups of two to four children. It's often accompanied by talk in which children describe their actions, making it easier for everyone to agree on the plot and characters. This is often tricky. Grandparents and parents may notice that these negotiations take longer than playing out the entire scene. (You might tell your grandpa or baby sister what role you want them to play—but you can't tell your older siblings or friends and know they'll obey.)

Between the ages of four and six, children's pretend play episodes are often longer and involve more players. Many grandparents have told me that they become totally engrossed watching grandchildren play out complex fantasies without costumes or props. Like Minka, children become skilled at using gestures and intonation to mark the transformations in their pretend roles. These fantasies can include a large cast of changing characters and plots that abound with conflicts, twists, and turns that astonish their grandparents.

At this age, although children still love playing with grand-parents, they're even more interested in playing with their friends. Friends share the same fascination with themes of power, life and death, and magic. Children's fantasies highlight the uncertainties in their desires, like the desire for both independence and adult protection.

These are years when superheroes, villains, space aliens, princesses, wizards—and fairies—take center stage, evoking archetypes of good and evil. We grandparents certainly don't bring the same degree of emotional charge to these themes as friends do!

Throughout these years, the joy children feel in imaginative play fosters powerful links to others. Their desire for a sense of wonder and joy motivates them to move beyond their own point of view to include the perspective of others. Children begin to see themselves from multiple perspectives as they take more complex pretend roles and coordinate those roles with others. As a result, children experience the joy of deeper connections with family and friends.

How Grandparents Can Encourage Rich Imaginative Play

We enjoy watching and taking part in our grandchildren's imaginative play. But sometimes we wonder when to step back or how to participate without stifling a child's imagination. Which materials and toys support more imaginative play? Which toys should be avoided? For example, grandparents wonder how to respond when they think play has become too violent or when a kindergartner plays out the same story again and again each day.

There's no easy recipe for every child or situation, but it's useful to think about two things that impact children's pretend play:

- The materials and toys available for play
- Our interactions with grandchildren in their pretend play

Materials and Toys That Support Rich Imaginative Play

Although children begin to engage in imaginative play as older toddlers or young preschoolers, most grandparents and parents introduce make believe soon after birth. Think of the baby games we play that involve pretense, clapping games like Pat-a-Cake or finger plays like the Itsy Bitsy Spider and bouncing games like horsey rides. We can play these pretend games anytime. No toys needed.

When toddlers first begin to pretend, they prefer common objects they know, like spoons and containers. They use spoons to "feed" their doll or stuffed animal, or a baby blanket to cover their "baby" and put it to sleep. No toys are needed for this— simple household objects are perfect.

Toys that are realistic replicas of familiar things can expand the themes of toddlers' imaginative play. Toys and materials like kitchen items and baby dolls or other replicas often cue the child to play out particular kinds of stories or themes. Miniatures of people, dogs, horses, pigs, cows, and cars inspire particular kinds of stories. Other favorites include trucks, cars, fire engines, and wagons large enough for toddlers to add a miniature person or cargo before zooming off to deliver a package or fight a fire.

What materials and toys support rich imaginative play for our older preschool and kindergarten grandchildren? At this age, grandchildren's ability to symbolize increases rapidly from ages three to six. An object no longer has to look like what the child intends it to symbolize. Now children can use any object for whatever they need in their pretend play.

The best materials and toys for older three, four, and five-year-olds are ones that teachers call *unstructured*. These include items like blocks of all sorts, scarves and capes for dressing up, old sheets to make spaces to hide away, and outdoor materials like pebbles, sticks, and acorns. At this stage, an object's meaning lives more in the child's imagination than in the object itself. Knowing this helps us grandparents pick out materials and toys that support richer pretend play instead of toys that may lead to repetitive or aimless play.

Dr. Diane Levin, a professor of human development and early childhood education at Boston University, has written many books on topics of great interest to teachers of young children and to families as well. Her recent books include *Teaching Young Children in Violent Times*, *Beyond Remote Concern Childhood*, and *So Sexy, So Soon*.

Years ago, Diane and several colleagues started TRUCE (Teachers Resisting Unhealthy Children's Entertainment), a national group of educators concerned about the negative impacts that some of today's toys, films, and video games can have on young children's behavior, play, and learning. Each year, TRUCE publishes excellent play and toy guides that help parents and educators support play in homes, schools, and communities.

The guides include tips on how to choose toys wisely as well as how to avoid toys that can harm children's play and development. These guides on the TRUCE website are free to download and reproduce. For years, I've recommended them to early childhood students, teachers, and parents. Now I'm delighted to also recommend them to grandparents. The information in the tips box below is taken directly from the guides (see also www.truceteachers.org).

Tips for Choosing Toys of Value

Toys have high play value when they ...

➤ Can be used in many ways.

➤ Allow children to be in charge of their play.

➤ Appeal to children at more than one age or level of development.

➤ Can be used with other toys for new and more complex play.

➤ Will stand the test of time and continue to be part of play as children develop new interests and skills.

➤ Promote respectful, non-stereotyped, non-violent interactions among children.

➤ Help children develop skills important for future learning and a sense of mastery.

➤ Can be used by children to play alone, as well as with others.

➤ Can be used by children of all ages, regardless of gender. (p. 4)

(cont.)

Tips for Choosing Toys of Value (cont.)

Avoid toys that ...

➢ Are linked to video games, computers, TV or movies dictating a play script rather than allowing children to develop their own ideas.

➢ Can only be used in one way, encouraging all children to play the same way.

➢ Look exciting but quickly become boring because they only require children to push a button and watch what happens.

➢ Do the playing "for" children, instead of encouraging exploration and mastery.

➢ Lead children to spend more time with TV or other media, letting the screen take control of their play.

➢ Lure children into watching the TV program or other media which is linked to the toy.

➢ Promote violence and sexualized behavior, which can lead to aggressive and disrespectful play.

➢ Separate girls and boys with highly gender-divided toys.

➢ Introduce academic concepts at too early an age, leaving less time for creative play that best prepares children for academic learning. (p. 7)

Grandparents often talk with each other about toys they recommend and toys to avoid. Some grandparents told me they've gone to local stores and found separate aisles for girls and boys. They're sometimes shocked to notice that even little kids know the difference. Girls head to the girls' aisle and boys to the boys' aisle. I remember these different aisles from when my own children were young—but now some trends are more extreme.

TRUCE highlights several toy trends that are particularly harmful.

1. Beware of toys that look like automatic combat weapons like AK-47s as well as toys with ties to violent media characters that can encourage aggressive, violent play.

2. Look out for the many toys for girls that make sexiness and appearance the focus of play.

3. Avoid toys that promote consumerism. The purpose of some toys seems to be to entice children to collect them all.

With so many toys on the market, ask yourself if the toy fits into one of these categories of toys. If it does, consider another choice.

Grandparents' Interactions with Their Grandchildren Can Encourage Rich Imaginative Play

As grandparents, we want to encourage our grandchildren's imagination and support their initiative. What are they pretending? What are they doing and why? We need to be keen observers. Only then can we begin to understand make believe from the child's point of view.

Looking closely below the surface of play is especially important when a child seems distraught or when we think play is becoming too aggressive. Then it's time to decide whether to stand back and give a child time to work it out, or whether it's time to step in and decide how we'll handle the situation.

Though it's so much fun to play with our grandchildren, we want to make sure that we don't get so caught up in the play that we begin interfering or taking control. When we override their initiative, our grandchildren feel less involved and less free to imagine. It's helpful to consider just how we interact with our grandchildren as they play.

Luca is outside with her toy dog and giraffe. Grandma Leni observes as Luca gives her animals some leaves from the privet bush, and murmurs "mmm ... mmmm" as she feeds them.

Audrey loves playing pretend with her Grandma Elaine. Today, they're heading off to the park for a picnic. Audrey gathers her babies (dolls and stuffed animals) and carefully "clicks" them into their car seats.

Kiera (five years) and her sister Camille (three years) are making believe they're witches. Kiera whispers, "You need to take this invisibility powder so the scary monsters can't see you." This is too scary for Camille, who tears up and runs to their grandmother Lenore who hugs her and turns to Kiera, "You and your friends like playing scary monsters, but Camille doesn't like it now. You could ask Camille if she still wants to play witches or play something that's not scary."

These stories show that sometimes our role is indirect, as when Leni stands nearby but doesn't hover and silently watches Luca feeding her animals. Our role in pretend play is often direct, as when Elaine participates in Audrey's play of taking her babies to a picnic. This is a good example of how a grandparent encourages a child's initiative and imagination by following the child's lead.

And at times our role is more directive, as when Lenore steps in to address Camille's distress with the suggestion of how to change the story line. Being aware of these different choices opens up a wider range of possibilities to support our grandchildren's rich imaginative play.

Subtle, indirect interactions can also support rich dramatic play. Like Leni, grandparents often prepare the environment and put out materials (like putting a baby bath outside on the grass) and encourage our grandchild's additions.

We also support children's dramatic play when we remove clutter or offer other props. For example, Angelo's two grandchildren are making believe that they're construction workers and have been building a town with blocks. After about an hour, Angelo notices that blocks are strewn about. The children can't find the blocks they need and don't have enough clear space. Without comment, he picks up scattered blocks and sorts some into piles.

Sometimes a grandparent takes a direct role by helping a grandchild join the play of others. This is a delicate dance. We must avoid wielding adult power and need to protect the other children's desire to continue their group's theme or story.

Arriving at the park, Sylvie follows her three-year-old grandson Jean-Paul to the sandbox. He stands by the side of the sandbox, holding his pail and watching two children make mountains. Carefully, he steps into the sand and walks over to watch them. Sylvie notices Jean-Paul and the

(cont.)

(cont.)

children looking at one another silently. After a moment, she intervenes by saying matter-of-factly, "Hi. It looks like Jean-Paul wants to play with you. He likes to build mountains, too. Can you make space for him?" The children look up at Jean-Paul and move over. Without a word, Jean-Paul joins the construction team.

Another challenge is knowing when to help children resolve conflicts. Offering calm, thoughtful suggestions can not only help play continue but also help children enrich their play. For example, if children are fighting over a car or who will be the driver, their grandparent might offer another car or suggest another appealing role, perhaps as the navigator with a GPS.

When imaginative play is long and complex, grandparents often interact with children in several ways within the same episode. Think of Ann and Minka's fairy café in the opening story of this chapter. Ann plays a supportive role as she helps Minka build a cubby house. Together, they scramble about to find the materials and work until it's completed.

When the café opens, Ann becomes a participant in Minka's dramatic play as she assumes the role of one of the customers in Minka's story. Throughout the afternoon, Ann's participation helps Minka stay focused and overcome frustrations. Minka's pretend play ends in smiles for the whole family.

CHAPTER 6

The Essential Benefits
of Outdoor Play

Outdoors, children's exuberance and boundless energy are on full display. They are less constrained than they are indoors, and their play is freer, multifaceted, more creative. Outdoors, they can move their whole bodies and exercise large muscles in boundless space. Unconfined, they can choose to be alone or with others, to be quiet or boisterous.

One moment they may enjoy stealthily collecting leaves behind the bush, all by themselves. The next, they may join other children galloping across a field, shouting with glee. Outdoors, children feel a part of nature as they run through fall leaves, lift their heads to feel the breeze ruffling their hair, or watch squirrels gathering seeds. Picture this outdoor scene:

Nelson and his daughters, Maryum (3 years) and Abril (11 months), arrive at a park next to San Francisco Bay, a scenic area with walking and bike trails, picnic tables, and benches alongside the water. Maryum clutches her kite, eager to release it. She's asked her dad to go to this particular park because she often watches people flying kites there. Now she'll be one of them!

After walking to an open space a little way up the slope of a hill, they put down their blanket. Lifting Abril into a baby carrier so his hands are free, Nelson helps Maryum attach the string then lays the kite with its colorful tail on the grassy slope. He shows her how to hold the kite so it's upright, and how to let it go.

Nelson: "Maryum, you hold up the kite and I'll start counting. When I say 'one,' run as fast as you can. When I say 'two,' let the kite go. I'll let out more string and we'll see if it goes up." After several failed attempts, the kite finally ascends. Maryum gallops after it, gaining speed as she runs down the slope, waving her arms as if she, too, was trying to fly.

Soon, they are joined by Abuelita Amparo whom Maryum calls "Lita," a close friend and neighbor. Maryum runs to tell Amparo to watch them fly the kite. With Amparo here, Nelson puts Abril on the blanket so she can crawl around. A moment later, Abril crawls off the blanket and grabs and pulls on several wild mustard flowers. Abril reaches up and Amparo helps her to standing. They walk slowly together, touching the plants.

Maryum and Nelson spend a few moments watching as several regulars at the park fly kites. The colorful kites swoop, swirl, and fly high above them. When Maryum says she wants to try something else, Nelson unties the tail from the kite and gives it to Maryum. She dashes up and down the slope, holding the bright pink, orange, and green kite tail above her head, and watches as it dances in the wind.

Suddenly, they hear loud honking. All four turn toward the water to see a flock of geese flying by. Maryum also notices several ground squirrels running among the large boulders that line the waters' edge. She looks up at her dad who nods, signaling that she can go watch the squirrels.

Running down, she climbs nimbly around a boulder until she has a clear view of two squirrels. She stands silently, watching the squirrels pick up seeds until their cheeks are round and full. Then they disappear into one of several nearby holes in the ground. Maryum runs back to her dad, intent and curious: "Why are they so small? ... Are they still babies? ... Where do the seeds come from? ... Do all the squirrels live down there?"

In this busy scene, we see all three key dimensions of outdoor play—the power of physical activity, activities that children initiate themselves, and the joy of nature play for the whole family. We can imagine Maryum's delight in her first attempts at kite flying. This is a special time with her dad as they try to figure out how to get her kite to fly.

After she notices the ground squirrel, she takes the initiative. With her dad's permission, she confidently runs off to observe them closely. She then returns eager to share her observations and questions.

In this scene, Abril starts off confined in a baby carrier. With the arrival of Amparo, a family friend she knows well, Abril is free to move about physically and explore together, feeling what it's like to be outside and active, feeling the earth, touching the plants, and watching the birds.

Essential Benefits of Outdoor Play

Pediatricians, educators, and developmental scientists emphasize that outdoor play is essential for children's development. Young children need outdoor time for play that is physically active and self-initiated. They also need to play in natural environments.

- **Physically active outdoor play:** Outdoor play that is physically active helps children develop strength and coordination. It also helps them develop kinesthetic awareness—the sense of the position and movement of their bodies.

- **Child-initiated outdoor play:** Outdoor play provides children opportunities to initiate play both by themselves and with others.

- **Outdoor nature play:** Children need many opportunities to play outdoors to develop the deep connections with nature that are critical in the early years.

As grandparents, many of us treasure childhood memories of hours playing outdoors. Unfortunately, children today spend less time playing outdoors than they did just a decade ago—certainly less than our generation did. And at the very time we're learning more about the importance of outdoor play, that play has shifted inside. Play has become less active and less social. Too often, play time equals screen time.

Why is this happening? Many childcare and preschool programs set aside little time for outdoor play. Instead, children sit at tables for hours, working on unimaginative, preplanned lessons that have little to do with their interests. At home, families may find there's little time for children to play outside or no one available to supervise. Parents often work long hours, arriving home just in time to make dinner and start bedtime routines.

Many families also worry about neighborhood safety. Others are concerned that playing outside carries too much risk of injury. For most young children, being outdoors means organized sports and other activities organized by adults, instead of play they initiate themselves.

The outdoors holds endless fascination for young children. When children have to stay inside, we often see them looking out the window, yearning to be outside. How fortunate for everyone when grandparents are available to come to the rescue!

Physically Active Outdoor Play

Aerobic activities support children's endurance by increasing their heart and breathing rates. Children strengthen their muscles when they play on jungle gyms, ride trikes, or climb trees. They strengthen their bones when they walk, run, and gallop, and lug around heavy play equipment.

The Centers for Disease Control and Prevention (CDC) recommend that children have at least 60 minutes per day of strenuous or moderate physical activity that includes aerobic activities, muscle-strengthening activities, and bone-strengthening activities.

Don't these recommendations sound familiar? We grand-parents know that aerobic, muscle-strengthening, and bone-strengthening activities are essential for our own health. And as we get older, avoiding falls requires maintaining our kinesthetic awareness.

Lists of recommended physical activities for older adults include walking, running, hiking on uneven trails, gardening, cycling, exercising with weights, and balancing. We can *feel* the health benefits of the active time we spend outdoors, whether walking with friends, gardening, cycling, or hiking. Playing outdoors provides *all* of us—grandparents as well as grandchildren—the necessary aerobic, muscle and bone-strengthening, and kinesthetic activities of a great workout.

Adult Guidance for Playground Safety

The American Academy of Pediatrics (AAP) website healthychildren.org provides an excellent resource on outdoor safety. The AAP reminds us that:

> *Even on the safe, age-appropriate playgrounds, adult guidance and supervision is the best way to prevent injuries. In fact, researchers say that lack of supervision is linked with nearly half of playground-related injuries. So, as your child climbs, slides, swings and glides, keep an eye on the action and be ready to intervene if they are using the equipment inappropriately! (Gilchrist, 2018)*

The following is my summary of two of AAP's key points on general playground safety:

1. **Check what's underneath.** Make sure that play yard surfaces made out of bark, chip, or artificial materials are sufficiently deep (three or more inches) and resilient so children won't be injured. Be aware that grass doesn't absorb impact and that hard surfaces like asphalt and concrete are never safe.

   The AAP points out that every year, many children seek treatment in emergency departments for playground-related injuries due to falls on surfaces that are too hard to protect children from the impact.

2. **Size it up.** Make sure that all equipment is appropriate for young children and in good shape.

   - **Climbing structures.** Platforms higher than 30 inches are dangerous for children under six years of age. Make sure the platforms have adequate guardrails, and double check for openings large enough for children to fall through. Check also for nails, screws, or dangerous edges or protrusions that children—or their clothes—could become caught on.

- **Slides.** Teach children to always go down slides feet first both to prevent head injuries and to avoid collisions by making sure other children are not on the slide. AAP reminder: Don't go down the slide with a child. Though it may seem helpful or safe to do so, research shows sliding in pairs leads to injuries.

- **Swings.** Teach young children to swing safely and know that jumping off or swinging on their tummies is dangerous. Be alert to make sure that other children and adults don't wander into the path of the swing—or your path if you're helping a child. Check for adequate clearance—swings should not be close together, and objects such as walls and fences should be at least six feet away from either side of the swing.

You can find the link to the Gilchrist (2018) article in the Resources list at the end of this book.

There are few resources on safety especially for grandparents. Above all, be aware that it takes us longer to respond than when we were parents. This is usually due to our longer reaction times, poorer balance, and, unless we see our grandchildren often, our inability to anticipate what they might do.

The following tips for grandparents are based on AAP guidelines and my own observations and experience:

- **Playground structures.** Some structures are small enough for young children but have platforms without railings two or more feet off the ground. That's unsafe not only for young children, who can fall or hurl themselves off, but also for grandparents who rush to catch them.

- **Swings.** Be alert and stay out of the way. Exercise judgment when pushing, especially in response to our grandchild's pleas of "higher, higher!"

- **Slides.** To catch or not to catch—that is the question. Are you limber enough? Is your back strong enough to catch a grandchild who comes flying down the slide at a racer's pace?

- **"Watch your back."** Too much lifting or lifting improperly can lead to back pain and serious injuries. Also be aware of how many times you lift your grandchild each day—in and out of the stroller, swing, climber, and so on. Think about how you can lift more safely and less often.

Child-Initiated Outdoor Play

Recently, I met with Dr. Jane Perry, internationally known for her research, advocacy, and writing on young children's outdoor play. Jane said that educators and grandparents' perspectives on play differ significantly. Educators need to have a rationale for play that they can share easily with families. Grandparents don't need to explain—they know that playing outside is just plain fun. As Jane explained:

Just being outside invites children to invent their own themes and roles. Grandparents might be especially interested in the way that children discover open-ended natural materials that can become anything in their play. Wood chips can be money. An acorn cap can be a fairy cup. And, of course, sand and water can be mixed together into whatever a grandchild's imagination calls forth.

Active outdoor play can give grandparents a wider window into their grandchildren's social and emotional experiences. It's a chance to watch and think about how grandchildren play, what they try to do, how they use the play spaces, alone and together.

I think grandparents will find that outdoor play has social, cognitive, and artistic as well as physical dimensions—and important challenges for young children. Grandparents can set up imaginative play spots—"this is where the dinosaurs live," "here is where you can cook"—so children can explore, follow their own initiative, and engage socially. It's a special time that grandparents share with their grandkids, and also a time when children's focus often shifts from playing with their grandparents to playing with their peers.

Children are naturally motivated to play together and want to be a friend. We find this in their attempts to keep their play going—children typically use their highest cognitive and language abilities when they play with their peers. For example, in order to join in a pretend story line, children have to problem solve as they figure out how and what to play with their playmates.

When children play together, the many conflicts and scrapes that naturally arise necessitate flexible thinking and negotiating so that their play can continue. Taking small risks is a necessary foundation for self-confidence. Many examples of appropriate risk taking occur in play, especially play that is outdoors and freely chosen and directed by kids. I think that grandparents may know this based on their lifetime of experiences.

I asked Jane for tips on how grandparents can support children's appropriate risk taking. Offering examples from her many years as teacher and research coordinator at the University of California, Berkeley, Harold Jones Child Study Center, she emphasized that the first step is for grandparents to understand that children experience great challenges in their everyday play—emotionally, socially, physically, and cognitively.

Jane gave the example of four-year-old Mollie playing outdoors. Mollie showed growing physical development in her fast-paced movement across rugged tanbark, while noticing her own improved coordination and her pleasure and interest in physical activity:

> *Mollie uses an imaginative way to convey displeasure about her lack of coordination and frequent stumbles: "I'm very slow right now because I'm a turtle." Later, as she becomes more coordinated, her growing sense of physical security is once again expressed imaginatively: "But right now I'm a lion." Running around the climber, she proclaims her sense of empowerment: "Sometimes I pounce on twigs because I'm a meat eater." (Perry & Branum, 2009, pp. 204–205)*

Mollie's new abilities enhance her confidence. She goes from a turtle to a lion, celebrated for its power, speed, and dominance in the wild. Now she feels ready to join in lion-like, vigorous, fast-paced peer play.

Outdoor social play involves fast-paced routines—like galloping as a group simply for the sheer joy of running. These fast-paced routines help children feel connected as they run together in fun chase games. Jane finished up our conversation with this advice for grandparents:

> *Children appreciate a grandparent's love and encouragement and benefit from a grandparent's imagination and sense of fun. When grandparents are relaxed and embracing of their grandchildren's efforts, children will thrive in a mutually loving relationship where their confidence and skills are celebrated.*

Outdoor Nature Play

Whether we live in the country, a small town, or a big city, we and our grandchildren can deepen our connections with the natural world. As we roam together, we find beauty in the color of local flowers, the call of local birds, the curl of the tiniest new leaf, and the majesty of an old tree.

For young children, deepening connections with nature usually means starting outside their front door to explore the nearby environment. Children need ample time to wander if they are to develop feelings and knowledge about the natural world as they see, hear, smell, and touch their surroundings.

The story that begins this chapter allows us to picture Maryum and her family at the water's edge, gazing skyward as geese fly by. We understand Maryum's fascination with ground squirrels as:

> She stands silently, watching the squirrels pick up seeds until their cheeks are round and full. Then they disappear into one of several nearby holes in the ground. Maryum runs back to her dad, intent and curious: "Why are they so small? ... Are they still babies? ... Where do the seeds come from? ... Do all the squirrels live down there?"

Childhood is a critical time for children to develop a relationship with the natural world. The North American Association for Environmental Education (NAAEE) emphasizes that children "who respect the environment feel an emotional attachment to the natural world, and deeply understand the link between themselves and nature, will become environmentally literate citizens" (NAAEE, 2016, p. 4).

The NAAEE advises that adults let children follow their natural curiosities. I see grandparents doing this all the time. These are special moments for grandparents, too, when they see their grandchild gently hold a worm and examine it, then return it to its habitat, or plant a seed in a jar on the window sill and watch it grow.

Each summer Luca (now five years old) and her big sister Ada travel cross country to stay with their grandparents who live on a lake. They spend these weeks with their cousins Remy and Reese who are about the same age, as well as their parents, aunts and uncles, and family friends. The four cousins fill their days with swimming, making hideaways, searching for treasures, and boating with their grandparents.

Their aunt Lisa sent me a short video of Luca waist-deep in water at the edge of the lake, reaching up to pick blueberries from bushes that arced over the water. Her face and hands were streaked with earth and the deep blue shade of the berries, and her laugh showed her brilliant blue teeth. Later Lisa called to tell me that they'd read *Blueberries for Sal* while eating their homemade blueberry cobbler.

Moments that forge strong bonds with nature happen anywhere. It's helpful when we look for opportunities closer to home.

Recently, Derek and I took Ava and Jake for a morning walk to check out one of our favorite places—our neighbor Meeta's garden with colorful flowers in bloom and edible herbs and vegetables surrounding a small pond with a metal frog that both children love to touch. Meeta was working in her garden, her small dog lying in the shade. She beckoned the children to stroll the path and held up lavender and mint for them to smell. She knelt down by Jake and held his hand so he could pat her dog. She snipped pieces of mint for Ava to smell, including peppermint, Moroccan mint, and lemon bergamot mint, and—to Ava's delight—gave her some chocolate mint so Ava could make tea for us when we got home.

Reading books can extend children's connections with nature and the outdoors. Have you noticed that so many of children's favorite books are set outside? Of course, children's books are often about animals, hence the outdoor settings, but so are many books about children's adventures. Perhaps it's because children—and authors and illustrators—love the outdoors.

Libraries have scores of excellent nature-themed books. Consider *Owl Moon* by Jane Yolen, *Gator, Gator, Gator!* by Daniel Bernstrom, *Box Turtle at Long Pond* by William T. George, *Hiking Day* by Anne Rockwell, and *Swimming with Seals* by Maggie De Vries about a girl who lives with her gran and great aunt. For kindergartners, *The Boy Who Drew Birds* by Jacqueline Davies is an engaging introduction to the National Audubon Society.

Be aware, however, that some popular children's book illustrations show animals in ways that are romanticized or cartoonish. Instead, extend children's interest and knowledge with books of nature photos.

Grandparents Reflect on Outdoor Play

I asked other grandparents about their favorite outdoor places to spend time with their grandchildren. A common response was backyards and leisurely walks in the neighborhood. Next were parks with play equipment designed especially for younger children. However, most fondly remembered were times spent in natural spaces, including larger city parks and trips to scenic places near lakes, rivers, and oceans, or hills and mountains.

How do these different outdoor environments support physically active play, child-initiated play, and nature play for our grandchildren as well as for us grandparents?

Many grandparents I spoke with talked about neighborhood walks as a special social time. It's a time when they feel both emotionally and physically connected as they walk together holding a child's hand or carrying an infant. They view these walks as occasions for children to learn about their neighborhood and enjoy the sights and sounds of their surroundings.

These are times to watch people at work, speak with neighbors, and play with a neighbor's dog. These are times when children can set the pace, follow their interests, and initiate activities. During these walks, everyone is physically active. Walking not only contributes to bone strength but also involves (to a lesser extent) aerobic and muscle-strengthening activities.

For toddlers, walking develops their kinesthetic sense and coordination as they bend down, kneel and stand up, and move as quickly as they can. Preschoolers and kindergartners run and hop or ride their scooters or bikes—activities that raise their heart rates and help develop their kinesthetic sense, balance, and coordination.

Some grandparents talk of neighborhood walks as times to feel connected with nature, not wild nature, but "neighborhood" nature. These are times to see the sky and feel the breeze and warmth of the sun, to gaze down at insects on the sidewalk and look up at birds. These are times to enjoy talking about trees and grasses, seeds and flowers, butterflies and birds, as well as neighborhood dogs and cats.

Grandparents take grandchildren to playgrounds for the children's sake, to encourage them to be physically active, learn new skills, and play with other kids. Playgrounds for young children have swings, climbers, and large sand areas where children can slide down slides and climb structures that are just the right size.

Grandparents choose playgrounds with safe baby swings when their grandchildren are infants and toddlers, or low swings so preschoolers can rock back and forth by themselves. Most grandparents said they knew of several playgrounds and sometimes chose a particular one that was good for kicking a soccer ball or one with pathways so kids could ride trikes, scooters, or bikes.

Grandparents talked about trips to large natural spaces as a special treat. They look forward to being in nature themselves and love sharing this time with family members, especially their grandchildren. They also enjoy seeing their grandchildren physically active for long periods, playing with other children, engaging in pretend play outside, and being outside in nature.

They pointed out that open spaces are popular with people of different ages, places where generations spend time together. Several emphasized how "lively and very alive" they felt in parks with large open spaces and treasure opportunities to explore them with their grandchildren.

After listening to these grandparents, I thought their experiences and opinions would interest readers and give them ideas for thinking about their own experiences. I was curious to discover for myself how these three different environments would engage our grandchildren and support their play and our own.

A Neighborhood Walk

We took the children for a typical neighborhood walk. Ava took her scooter along and Derek walked with Jake. Almost immediately, Ava spied a snail beside the walkway. Just as she bent down to look at it more closely, Jake picked it up. "Jake, be careful. Be gentle," Ava cautioned, and he was.

We walked slowly, looking for more snails, when Jake started babbling excitedly. Picking up a quartz stone from the narrow strip between the sidewalk and the street, he held it up for Derek to see. The stone sparkled in the sunlight. "Look what you discovered!" Derek exclaimed. Jake walked on, carrying his treasure and holding it up often for us to see.

By this time, Ava was eager to get going. She headed down the block on her scooter while I walked quickly beside her. Ava turned around and scooted several times to Jake and Derek, and then back to me until we were all at the corner. She'd made great progress in the weeks since I'd first seen her ride and could keep the scooter pointing straight ahead instead of drifting from side to side.

We circled the block and found Jake and Derek watching intently as city workers jackhammered a section of sidewalk. Soon, Jake tired of watching and Ava decided that she was finished riding her scooter. Time to head for home.

A Special Playground for Young Children

A mile from our grandchildren's home is a playground with a fenced area for infants and children up to six years old. I watched several children freely run, hop and skip, climb play structures, slide down the slide, throw and catch balls, and lug around heavy buckets of wet sand to make "mountains" in the sand pit.

Jake and another toddler ran awkwardly from the slide to the sand area. Ava sat side by side on the swings with another girl she'd just met, talking companionably as they pumped up and down by themselves.

Time at this park with its small, fenced area for young children was quite different from our neighborhood walk. I could see that the park was planned to encourage children's physical activity, particularly aerobic, muscle-strengthening, and bone-strengthening activities.

The park's design also promotes children's social interactions. The large sand area encloses smaller areas that provide cozy spaces for two or three children. The large play structure features a slide. Next to the slide is a low platform with a pretend telescope and steering wheel so children can play alone or together while waiting for their turn on the slide.

What about grandparents? I noticed that grandparents spent most of their time observing and helping as needed. They were rarely physically active themselves in ways that might keep them fit. And, though everyone was friendly, there seemed less social interaction among grandparents and more phone conversations.

Natural Open Spaces

Derek and I took Ava and Jake to a large county park with lots of open space. Ava soon joined a group of several preschool and kindergarten children who were running, hopping and skipping, throwing balls and chasing after them.

In this natural space, children were climbing rocks and trees, balancing along a long tree root, running up and sliding down a grassy rise, and playing beside the shallow creek. Imitating his sister, Jake toddled up the small grassy rise, then happily stepped onto the fallen branch on top of the rise.

After about an hour, Derek, the children, and I walked over to one of the benches near the shallow creek to eat our picnic lunch. Several other families sat on nearby benches while their children played on the grassy bank of a small stream. After our lunch, Ava and Jake joined three of the children who were busy filling their buckets with small, wet pebbles, and helped them pile pebbles along the edge to construct their "river bank." Derek and

I joined their parents, watching and commenting on the fun the children were having together.

This large park with open spaces provides many options for children and adults, including grandparents. It offers numerous possibilities for young children to engage in physically active outdoor play—play they initiated themselves—and, naturally, nature play.

Derek and I noticed many multigenerational families. We watched young children and adults of different ages, including other grandparents and, possibly, great-grandparents. Most adults in this park seemed actively involved, far more so than at the park for children.

This park and the one where Maryum flew her kite with her dad are settings where children can also watch adults run around playing soccer or frisbee and riding bikes. We want our grandchildren to know that adults, as well as children, enjoy active play. Dr. Jane Perry sums it up well: "Playing outdoors is just plain fun!"

All of us hope our grandchildren will have wonderful memories of playing with us. A while ago, I asked some older children to tell me what they remember doing with their grandparents when they were little. Strikingly, most memories involved outdoor experiences, like a grandparent cheering them on as they raced down the block, or riding on a grandparent's shoulders, playing together at a nearby park, swimming, and hiking.

It seems that time spent together outdoors is not only fascinating at the moment but also has staying power, the power to create lasting memories.

CHAPTER 7

Sharing a Sense of Wonder
Science and Play

If a child is to keep alive his inborn sense of wonder, he needs the companionship of at least one adult who can share it, rediscovering with him the joy, excitement and mystery of the world we live in.
– Rachel Carson (1965, p. 55)

How marvelous for our grandchildren when we provide this special companionship. How marvelous for us to feel a sense of childhood wonder about the world. Our grandchildren are our special companions who share their drive to explore and discover.

As grandparents, we can look with youthful eyes as we jointly explore, ask questions, and seek new understandings. Whenever we're absorbed in playful activities, the problems and questions that engage us are our own—not "prefabricated" questions someone asks even though they already know the answer.

Grandchildren find these questions inherently interesting because they arise as they play. As this next story shows, together we are active, playful learners.

On this snowy but relatively warm day, Miguel is playing with his five-year-old twin granddaughters Breanna and Mikayla in the freshly fallen snow. They try to make snowballs, but the snow doesn't stick together. Miguel realizes that the snow is too fluffy. He waits to see what the girls will do next. Breanna and Mikayla take out their collection of sand toys— plastic pails and containers and whimsical molds shaped like animals. The three try to make animal shapes. Breanna is the first to lift the mold and uncover the shape—a horse. The shape immediately falls apart. "I know," she says, "you have to pack it more." They pack the snow with harder pats. Success!

Later the girls use the quart containers to make cakes. Soon they have an elegant row of five snow cakes decorated with pebbles.

Mikayla: "Let's take one inside and see what happens. How long will it take to melt?"

Breanna: "Grandpa, what will happen to the pebbles? How much water will it make?"

Miguel: "I'm not sure. Let's see."

They put a cake on an old tray. Miguel watches Mikayla and Breanna carry it with great care into the house and place it on the kitchen counter. They watch expectantly. It doesn't melt. Miguel suggests that they look at the clock and he'll help them see how long it takes. Mikayla and Breanna draw pictures while they wait and watch.

After 10 minutes, they notice a small amount of water collecting around the bottom of the cake. Little by little the puddle in the tray gets bigger and the cake gets smaller and the shape changes. Soon it doesn't look much like a cake any more. The lump takes more than an hour to melt.

How much water did it make? Mikayla suggests that to find out they could pour the water back in the plastic container. Miguel takes out a funnel, and Mikayla pours carefully, trying not to spill. The container is not even half full of water. What a surprise!

Breanna points out that the pebbles are no longer at the top but rather on the bottom of the container. Mikayla: "Let's take it back outside and see what happens. Maybe it will freeze again. Will it turn to ice?"

(cont.)

(cont.)

They take the container outside and pour the water and pebbles onto the snow beside the driveway. The water makes a rounded puddle in the snow that begins to flow in different directions. The pebbles stay on top of the snow. Mikayla and Breanna decide to show their "experiment" to their mom when she comes to pick them up. When she arrives several hours later, the children find the spot easily because the pebbles are still on top of the snow. The water has disappeared, but look—the snow under and around the pebbles is melted and shiny.

Exploring Together

When we watch our grandchildren play, we can understand why young children have been called natural scientists. Science is a crucial part of play, and learning about the physical world is what science is all about.

Scientists who have watched young children play point to many ways children are involved in science during their spontaneous explorations. Not many of us grandparents are scientists—but if we look at children's play from a more scientific perspective, we can appreciate the richness of our grandchildren's play and think of activities to enjoy together. We also realize that young children's play provides the foundation children need to be active science learners throughout their school years.

Throughout the afternoon, Breanna and Mikayla observe, explore, investigate, ask questions, and propose answers. Breanna designs a problem when she wonders why the horse shape falls apart and then suggests a hypothesis, "You have to pack it more."

Through their play, the children and their grandfather are learning more about the properties of snow and water. Mikayla and Breanna are forming initial understandings of important scientific concepts such as the transformation of matter—from snow, a solid, to water, a liquid. Miguel develops his own understandings of how matter is transformed as he ponders questions his granddaughters asked: "How much water will it make?" and "Let's take it back outside and see what happens. Maybe it will freeze again. Will it turn to ice?"

In this typical winter play scene, we see the children's curiosity about the physical world. Like scientists, Mikayla and Breanna display the disposition and drive to discover. Through play, grandparents and grandchildren experience science as a social, collaborative endeavor to learn about the world we live in.

Playful Explorations

What's a good environment for the fun of playful exploration and discovery? The best advice is to "start where you are"—literally! Where do you and your grandchildren play? What kinds of play occur outdoors as well as inside? What are your grandchildren's current interests and your own? What play activities are their favorites? Though it's fun to go to special places and do special things, start by exploring and discovering opportunities for play in familiar settings.

Children's playful explorations not only occur over several hours of play (like playing in the snow) but also in more fleeting play.

Fred's granddaughter Gracie has just awakened from a nap. He knows this is a time when she prefers gentle movements and slower rhythms, and so Fred just observes as Gracie reaches to touch Curly, the stuffed toy dog he's holding. She pats Curly's back with her fingers and then, with her whole hand, rubs the fur back and forth along Curly's paw. Gracie grasps Curly more firmly, pulls him toward her, and rubs her face against him.

Fred sees that when a front paw touches her lips, Gracie sucks on it for a moment, then moves it away from her face. He's surprised at how long she gazes intently at the paw. Then looking up at Fred, she moves the dog toward him and places it against his hand. Fred takes it and moves it back toward Gracie: "Hi, Curly! Hi, Gracie!"

How does this loving, playful interaction relate to science? Gracie uses her sense of touch as she pats and rubs Curly's fur against her cheek and lips. She is also exploring texture, how Curly feels, by sucking on his paw. His fur is silky smooth, and the stuffing in his paw retains its shape when she sucks on it.

From early infancy, we see children using all their senses—touching, tasting, smelling, seeing, and hearing—to explore their immediate environment. In Gracie's actions we see the beginnings of explorations and scientific inquiry. Fred is delighted when Gracie reaches toward him and puts Curly against his hand. She seems to be initiating a second round of this new game—and a new phase of discovery.

Here's an example of how a simple shopping trip merges with play and the exploration of life cycles:

Every Thursday after preschool, three-year-old Eli stays with his grandmother Carrie. Today, Carrie has saved a trip to the garden nursery in anticipation of the fun she thinks they'll have. At the nursery, they shop for two cherry tomato seedlings to plant in containers on her patio. Carrie tells Eli that he can select the plants. Carefully observing, he walks slowly down the aisle.

Eli: "Look. They're so small, so tiny." He touches several leaves gently. "They're soft and furry." He bends over to smell them. "I like the way they smell ... What's this called?" he asks, pointing to the stem.

Carrie: "That part's the stem. The stem is straight up and down ... and see these thin little branches that grow off from the stem."

Eli: "Where are the tomatoes?"

Carrie: "That's a good question. You've just found tomato plants without tomatoes!"

Carrie realizes that, though Eli has asked such an obvious question, it's one she's never considered before. She wonders how to reply without diminishing his curiosity and interest by overloading him with information. She suggests a plan: "You can choose two plants. We'll plant these outside when we get back to my apartment. Then, every Thursday when you come over, we can watch to see where the tomatoes will grow."

In that moment, she gets an idea of a way to continue these moments together.

(cont.)

"Let's take a picture now of you with the plants," she says. "If you want, every time you come to my apartment you can water and watch the tomato plants. We can take a picture of you and the tomato plants every time, every week. And if you like, we can even make a photo book."

Carrie delights in and shares Eli's sense of wonder. As she watches Eli's eagerness to learn more, she thinks up a way to continue their adventure and support his scientific curiosity about how plants grow. She'll take pictures each week of her grandson and the tomato plants. Eli is her very special companion for rediscovering "the joy, excitement, and mystery of the world we live in."

Getting into the Spirit of Science

Like many grandparents, I have early memories of exploring my neighborhood. As a young child, I loved messing about with sand and water, finding snails in empty lots, and spending afternoons at a cousin's house building towns with blocks and cars. But science in elementary school was different and rarely interesting. There were too many facts to be memorized and five-step experiments to follow. It wasn't until I was in college and working in a lab that I rediscovered my fascination with science—my life took an unexpected turn. I ended up majoring in zoology, working in laboratories, and then becoming a science educator. In the 1960s, I spent a few years working with a team of scientists and educators to develop a new approach to teaching science in which children were actively engaged.

Best practices in science education have changed a lot since most grandparents were young. The American Association for the Advancement of Science (AAAS) provides guidance for science programs for students in kindergarten through second grade:

> *Getting into the spirit of science and liking science are what count most. Awareness of the scientific worldview can come later. (AAAS, Project 2061, Benchmarks for Science Literacy, 1993).*

Development takes time. This concept certainly applies to children before they go to kindergarten. The point is not to try to jump-start development. It makes no sense to try to make preschoolers into third graders. As we saw in Miguel's play with his granddaughters Breanna and Mikayla, grandparents can relax and enjoy the early years as a time for children to be themselves, free to explore and discover.

Whether or not we have a background in science, having fun with our grandchildren is our primary goal. We know that young children's approaches to discovery are not systematic, like those of scientists. But young children, grandparents, and scientists alike share the joy of discovery. Through play, grandparents contribute to their grandchildren's lives by supporting their grandchildren's interests and understandings.

As children explore their environment through play, they develop what science educators call "scientific dispositions." Scientific dispositions include curiosity, creativity, interest, and the drive to solve problems. These are definitely playful qualities that grandparents want to encourage.

The stories about Breanna, Mikayla, and Eli show that playing naturally leads young children to seek answers to their questions. They're engaging in what educators call *scientific practices* as they explore, observe, describe, compare, and speak with others about their ideas.

Through play, they develop the rich vocabulary they need to communicate their ideas: "That's not the right green. I need this crayon for the grass. What do you call this kind of green?" Play supports children's inquiry and discovery as they ask questions and seek answers. Mikayla suggests, "Let's take it [the snow] back outside and see what happens." She goes on to develop a hypothesis when she says, "Maybe it will freeze again."

Scientific concepts refer to the big ideas or organizing principles of science. Like scientists, young children develop these concepts over time as their understanding increases. Even toddlers begin to develop understandings of some scientific concepts that they can apply widely.

Take a concept like color. A blue plate. A blue hat. A dark blue book. A young child's realization that all these objects are blue involves understanding the concept of color. Color—in this case, blue—refers to a property these objects share.

As adults, we find some concepts highly complex while others, like color, seem simple to us—until we appreciate them from our young grandchild's point of view. As they play, children explore the objects in their environment. Children learn about the properties of familiar objects as they see their colors, feel their shapes and textures, and find that some are easy to lift but some are just too heavy.

Young children also develop early understandings of more complex concepts such as evaporation, acceleration, and the life cycle. Throughout elementary school, grandparents will see children developing more and more abstract scientific concepts.

As we watch our grandchildren play, we see them learn facts that relate to different fields of scientific study such as physics, biology, geology, astronomy, and chemistry as well as engineering and technology. *Scientific content* refers to factual scientific information. Grandparents help their grandchildren gain such information by encouraging them to follow their curiosity about things that interest them.

Luna's interest in ground squirrels makes her want to learn more facts about them as she builds a diorama of a ground squirrel habitat.

Felipe's interest in rocks leads him to identify and learn about the properties of the rocks he's collected nearby, including shale and sandstone.

Jimmy and his cousin Leilani make a drip sand castle. It's tall, with towers and surrounded by a moat in case a wave rolls in. As the sand in the towers begins to dry, one of them starts crumbling. Jimmy and Leilani know a lot about engineering with sand, especially the strengths and limitations of wet sand. Without a word, they add sand to make the tower wider and then more sand to buttress it.

Young children don't recognize artificial boundaries between science, engineering, and technology. Their play *always* includes engineering and technology as well as science—and so does our own play with them.

Science educators explain that the term *engineering* refers to what we do as we try to solve problems in a systematic way. Young children engage in engineering practices every day as they figure out how to swing by themselves, build sandcastles, race cars down a ramp, or build with blocks. "Grandpa, let's see if the bridge is stronger if we use that longer block across instead of this shorter one."

Technology refers to all the tools we develop and use, not just smartphones and computers. Think of the common tools we use as we ride a bike, play tennis or golf, prepare food, or work in the garden. Think about the tools young children use when they learn to eat with a spoon and fork or chopsticks, cut with scissors, or use a shovel to dig in the sandbox.

When I've talked with other grandparents about science, engineering, and technology, many explain that they never had the chance to develop deeper understandings of science, much less engineering or technology. But in fact, we don't need great expertise to feel confident helping our grandchildren explore and understand the natural world!

As we play together, observing and listening to our grand-children, we don't need to become experts. The stories in this chapter show that grandparents' everyday play supports children's developing scientific understandings. We can think of ourselves and our grandchildren as playful, creative, and curious investigators.

Tips for Exploring & Discovering Together

➢ Science educators recommend asking open-ended questions—"What are some things you could do with that?" Open-ended questions promote deeper thinking because they have many possible answers. In contrast, closed-ended questions have only one right answer.

➢ Ask real questions instead of questions you already know the answer to. "How did you blow that bigger bubble?" or "What did you see through your magnifying glass?"

➢ Share information that children cannot find out by themselves. For instance, naming a butterfly—"That's a monarch"—gives young children factual information they can't discover on their own.

(cont.)

➢ If you and your grandchild run out of ideas, you can take a walk outside and see what ideas and questions come up spontaneously.

➢ A search through drawers or cabinets might turn up balls of twine, masking tape, measuring cups, an old pulley, sandpaper, a kitchen scale, rubber bands, funnels, strainers, a potato masher, a mortar and pestle, collections of buttons, ribbons, empty spools from thread, or empty shoe boxes. These odds and ends offer so many possibilities you might not have connected with science or play!

Remember that exploration and discovery take time. When grandchildren are interested and deeply engrossed, their attention span is sometimes longer than our own. This is the perfect time for us to stand back, observe, and appreciate young children's interest in scientific endeavors. When your grandchild is focused and engaged, remember that asking a question can interrupt, be distracting, or unintentionally suggest that your interest is more important than following their own.

Grandparents' Stories of Exploring Together

In their spontaneous play, our grandchildren show us their interests, the questions they raise, and how they try to solve problems. As we explore and discover together, play takes us into the vast realms of science, engineering, and technology.

Playing with Water

Think about the inviting opportunities for investigations with water. Playing in the kitchen sink with warm soapy water, measuring cups, and spoons, or playing in the bath tubs with containers, sponges, and a few plastic toys. Or playing in the summer beside a river or at the beach—or in a toddler's wading pool.

When she was just a one-year-old, my granddaughter Zoë loved playing in the wading pool with her four-year-old brother Elijah. She would strike the water—making little splashes, big splashes—all the while shrieking with glee. Elijah might be busy pouring, filling, and emptying small containers. He'd hand her a container and put out his hand so she could pour the water on it. They'd push the containers down in the water and watch them pop up again. What floats? What sinks? What can we try—a leaf, a pebble, a twig? What a team of young scientists!

Playing with Light and Shadows

Grandchildren and grandparents all over the world delight in play and explorations with light and shadows. What memories do you have? Maybe you remember seeing your shadow on the sidewalk and noticing that sometimes it was taller and sometimes it was shorter? Do you remember using a flashlight to cast shadows on the wall? Or making up a shadow play with silhouettes as you stood behind a sheet?

I have vivid childhood memories of playing with light and shadows. Years later as a parent, I followed my children's interests and recalled many memories. Now, my grandchildren think up new possibilities and recreate the shadow play of their parents and grandparents. Together we've made all kinds of shadow animals that fly and galumph, and strange imaginary creatures with many hands, feet, and heads.

Inside, we've used flashlights to make shadows of everyone in the family. Outside, we've figured out the time of day and where to stand to make the tallest—and the shortest—shadow. We've used bright chalk to outline kids on trikes, kids holding balls, kids on skateboards, and outline our grandchildren twisting their shadows into "strange imaginary creatures."

Although young infants may delight in shadows, their under-standing of light and shadows emerges slowly, beginning during infancy and continuing through early childhood and then middle childhood and adolescence. Younger children don't understand that the shadow of the chair on the wall relates to the position of the chair. They usually think the object itself makes the shadow and not the fact that the chair blocks light from shining on the wall. Not until middle childhood do most children understand that shadows result from the absence of light.

For grandparents, it's captivating to see our grandchildren's play with light and shadows. These experiences form the foundation for their future understandings. We can support and participate in play with light and shadows by wordlessly watching a shadow together, offering props, and joining in the evolving play.

Investigating Physics, Engineering, and Technology

If scientists were to read the stories in this chapter, they might point out that as we play together, we often engage in activities related to physics, engineering, and technology. Children playing with water use tools like containers, funnels, and brushes. As they play, they become aware of properties of water such as buoyancy and transparency.

They observe transformations of matter as snow melts, water freezes, and water evaporates. Similarly, in their play with light and shadow, they engage in engineering and technology practices and solve problems as they figure out that an old bed sheet will make a good screen for their shadow play.

Play that involves operating vehicles on ramps is like an early childhood practicum for physics, engineering, and technology, and involves concepts like motion, velocity, and friction.

On Mary's most recent visit, she saw that her grandchildren now have an impressive collection of toy vehicles of all sizes, from small matchbox cars to a big fire truck. On this rainy day, they imagine the area rug is their city and drive their vehicles on roads made with strips of cardboard. Jackson asks Grandma Mary to help him cut a longer, heavier strip of cardboard so he can make a ramp from the high building (a hassock) down to the road. The ramp is ready, but when Jackson puts a little car on the ramp, it immediately rolls off the side. Mateo announces that he has an idea and heads off to search the recycling bin in the kitchen. He returns with his treasures—a long cardboard paper towel roll and two toilet paper rolls. Mateo and Mary hold the longer roll against the hassock and Jackson rolls the car. ZOOM! It works. Mateo increases the angle again and again. The car goes farther and zooms faster.

Living Things

Young children are particularly interested in living things and how they move, grow, and change. Think of Carrie's story about growing tomato plants with her grandson Eli or Luna's interest in ground squirrels. Of course, children are always especially interested in their own pets. I'm intrigued with young children's fascination with living things—and the pleasure I see grandparents take in sharing their grandchildren's interests.

What are your grandchild's interests and your own? Wherever you live, there are countless possibilities to explore together. Outdoors, children observe animals like birds, insects, worms, and snails. They discover they can find plants everywhere—growing wild in parks, by streams and lakes—and, in our garden, find weeds as well as the plants we grow intentionally.

Environmental educator David Sobel (2008) writes that it's vital for children to develop a "sense of place," the sense of themselves in connection to their surroundings no matter where they live. Sobel proposes that children's experiences in nature are essential for them to develop a deep love of nature and care for the environment.

How do young children develop a "sense of place"? What roles can grandparents play? To learn more, I spoke with Larry Malone, the co-director of the Full Option Science Study (FOSS), a widely used science curriculum for students in elementary and middle school. For many years, I've sought Larry's expertise about play and science for young children. Now, I asked him to speak as a longtime grandparent and suggest ideas to other grandparents.

Larry talked about how children develop a sense of place through pleasurable, everyday outdoor experiences with their grandparents. He gave examples from his own childhood.

He remembered holding his grandfather's hand and walking together through the fields of his grandparents' farm. He described his grandfather adjusting the irrigation system while explaining in simple terms how the system worked. I asked Larry if he considered that play. He emphasized what great fun it was then, and fun to remember it now. It was play, it was science and engineering, and it was a special time together.

Larry's advice for us grandparents is to help grandchildren develop a sense of place by spending lots of time outdoors and experiencing the elements—splashing in the puddles, running in the wind, raising their face to the falling snow. A person's sense of place continues to develop over time, throughout childhood and adulthood.

Larry finished our discussion by pointing out that time outside is not just time for us to talk to children about what we see. It's also a special time for us to listen carefully to what our grandchildren notice and enjoy getting to know them better as we see the world through their eyes.

Sharing a Sense of Wonder

There's a small park near my home that has a few benches near a small pond. It's perfect for when I feel like taking a break. Last fall, I was sitting there eating a snack when two women, about my age, asked if they could join me on the bench. Soon we were joined by seven others—two younger women and five young children who carried pails, scoopers, nets, large magnifying lenses, and homemade fishing poles without hooks and made out of branches and string. What a lively place this had become! It turned out that these were three generations—two grandmothers, each with her daughter and her daughter's young children who looked about three to six years old.

It was soon obvious that this was a favorite place for the children. Carrying their pails and nets, they ran along the edge of the pond sharing their observations. "Look at all the duckweed today!" "I just saw a mosquito fish. Now it's swimming over to you!" "Where? I don't see it ... oh, there." "And more, here!" "Do you remember when we saw the fish with the eggs in her belly?" "Look, that one's so little—maybe it just hatched—is that the mother there?"

"Let's look for snails."

Two children ran back to get their scoopers and began to scoop water into their nets, looking for snails. They found several tiny snails attached to the underside of the water plants and called to the adults to come and see. Immediately, one grandmother went over and bent down as the children shared their finds excitedly, pointing to the "baby snails."

When she said she couldn't see the snails, one child ran to get a magnifying lens. Everyone wanted a turn. This led to a great discovery—tiny jelly-like, translucent eggs attached to plants. Inside the eggs were miniscule snails. The children's gleeful cries of discovery brought their mothers and the second grandmother to join them, and a third grandmother—me.

Sometimes we're playing together outside—finding snail eggs in a pond, collecting rocks, or flying kites and paper airplanes. Sometimes we're playing inside, examining a collection of buttons or building a longer ramp for cars to zoom down. Sometimes we take a special trip to play in the mountains or a lake, a beach, or an aquarium.

Relatively few of us are scientists, but playing around with science, engineering, and technology happens everywhere. We and our grandchildren can share our curiosity and imagination. We give them a legacy when we become their companions in discovery. They share their childhood sense of wonder and bequeath us these precious moments.

THE GIFT OF PLAY

CHAPTER 8

Play, Problem Solving, and Children's Math

This rainy winter morning, Cathy and her grandchildren, two-year-old Seth and six-year-old Robert, are making oatmeal cookies for their afternoon snack. Together, they've measured and mixed the ingredients, and each has taken a generous portion of dough. Cathy tells the children it's time to add some special ingredients. She puts out handfuls of raisins, cranberries, and walnut pieces, then asks Seth and Robert for special requests. Seth asks for little pretzel sticks and some peanut butter. Robert suggests adding bananas and dates.

Cathy notices that Robert shapes his dough into a ball and is looking at the assorted ingredients. He takes a spoonful of peanut butter, using his fingers to mix it into the dough. Next, he breaks off a small piece of banana, mashes it with a fork, then adds it.

Slowly and carefully, Robert pats the dough into an irregular shape and sprinkles on a few raisins and cranberries. He kneads it, rolls it all together, and considers the growing ball of dough for a moment. Then he picks up some pretzel pieces and breaks two walnut halves into smaller pieces before reforming the ball carefully. "For my first one, I'm going to make a huge star," Robert announces, but he has difficulty flattening the dough into a star shape. He takes a smaller amount, rolls it up, and pats it down. "Look. It's an oval, not a circle," he observes.

Seth uses a different cookie-making strategy. He begins by forming the dough into two roughly equal handfuls, then divides each piece again. Lining up the four irregularly shaped pieces, he places them in a row and systematically pounds each flat, while chanting, "one, two, three, four, five, six." He examines them.

"This cookie is bigger," Seth says, looking at the first one, and then pinches off a small piece of dough. "What goes on this big one?" he asks himself aloud. Carefully picking out four raisins and a walnut piece, he presses them onto the dough. "What goes on this tiny one?" he asks himself as he picks up the second, smaller ball. He breaks a pretzel into three pieces and sticks them upright into the dough. "Three birthday candles," he declares, looking up at his brother and grandmother.

Robert and Cathy look at Seth and nod in agreement. "Good job," replies Robert, complimenting his younger brother's efforts. "Three birthday candles," echoes Cathy. "And," Seth announces, "I'm going to be three."

They return to cookie crafting. Twenty minutes later, all the dough has been transformed into cookies ready for the oven. For Cathy, Robert, and Seth, the fun of baking together and the aroma of warm oatmeal cookies may be remembered long after the cookies are eaten.

Cathy's story of baking cookies with her grandsons shows how playful and informal everyday activities provide opportunities to explore the mathematical dimensions of our world. Through play we enhance our grandchildren's natural interest in mathematics. Mathematics is a central part of young children's play. And not surprisingly, playfulness is central to mathematicians' own creative processes.

When we play with our young grandchildren, we are free to wander over the mathematical landscape through informal, creative activities. When they're older, children will be ready for the formal mathematics of their school years. The National

Association for the Education of Young Children (NAEYC) and the National Council of Teachers of Mathematics (NCTM) agree:

Throughout the early years of life, children notice and explore mathematical dimensions of their world. They compare quantities, find patterns, navigate in space, and grapple with real problems such as balancing a tall block building or sharing a bowl of crackers fairly with a playmate. Mathematics helps children make sense of their world. (NAEYC & NCTM, 2002, updated 2010, p. 1)

Whether or not we adults think we have strong abilities in mathematics, we do understand basic mathematical concepts. We often engage in mathematical thinking but may be unaware of the mathematical basis of everyday routines as we set the oven temperature or choose a container large enough for leftovers. We do this so automatically and probably don't recall the long, sometimes arduous process of how we developed important mathematical concepts.

Our grandchildren are interested in what we do, and many of our everyday activities involve mathematics. As they play, we sometimes hear our grandchildren echo what they've heard. Young-Sook, for instance, is pretending to make rice. She measures ingredients while repeating to herself, "One cup of rice, two cups of water." Soon she calls out, "Grandma, Grandpa, dinner's ready!"

The Mathematical Landscape

In everyday play, grandchildren deepen their under-standing of mathematical concepts that are the "big ideas" of mathematics—number sense, spatial relationships, and patterns. Today and even in elementary school, many children are taught these key concepts along with the formal names. When we grandparents were young, we certainly learned these basic concepts, but few of us were ever taught the names for them!

As grandparents, learning about these "big ideas" helps us deeply appreciate and support our grandchildren's developing abilities to explore the mathematical dimensions of their world.

Number Sense

Children begin using number names when they are two or three years old. Parents and grandparents are excited with this accomplishment but are often bewildered to find that children's use of numbers is so hit or miss. But keep in mind that most children only begin to use number concepts consistently and logically at 7–10 years old.

They first need to develop the ability to understand several related concepts that make up what educators call number sense. Number sense includes *number names*, *rote counting*, and *one-to-one correspondence*. We can look more closely at Cathy's story:

Seth knows he's broken the pretzel into three pieces ("three birthday candles"). He knows and recites the *number names* in order: "one, two, three, four, five, six." But Cathy notices that Seth doesn't actually have six objects. Similarly, when Seth chants, "one, two, three, four, five" as he flattens out four portions of dough, she sees that although he counts to five by rote (*rote counting*), he has four, not five cookies. It's helpful to realize that Seth has difficulty understanding amounts greater than three.

What does this mean for grandparents? I think it's important to know that children don't learn number concepts simply by hearing people count. Although Seth does know the English words for the number names of one, two, and three, he doesn't understand what they mean. Seth sees the pieces of dough, but he doesn't know the number of pieces. He can't yet match, or correspond, the number names with the number of pieces of dough he's counting (*one-to-one correspondence*).

In the weeks ahead, Cathy might notice Seth carefully touch each piece of dough as he counts them in order, "one, two, three." Have you seen a child doing this? When children count this way, they're using physical actions to match the number of objects with the corresponding number.

For many children, this is a big step forward in their understanding of one-to-one correspondence. After a while, they can look at three pennies on the table and tell us there are three pennies. But if we put down seven pennies, they may need to touch each one as they count.

It's helpful for us to understand that children need time to mature and engage in relaxed, playful experiences—and it's wonderful when we take pleasure in their mathematical accomplishments. The more we know, the more we will see.

As young children try to figure out an amount, we might notice that they use such words as "more," "less," "equal," and "the same." For example, Seth looks at the amount of dough he sees on his plate and compares it to the amount he sees on Robert's plate. He thinks that they don't have the same amount of dough and complains, "Robert has more than me." Seth asks for "some peanuts" and Robert wants "a few raisins." Teachers call these words quantifiers because they tell us "how many."

In fact, quantifiers like "more," "none," "some," "few," and "all" are some of the first number relationships young children recognize. That's quite an accomplishment! We also see two or three-year-old children estimating approximate amounts. Two-year-old Seth divides the dough into two pieces of about the same size. Notice that Seth uses the correct number to say how many: "Three birthday candles." Robert uses the correct number to indicate which one: "For my first one, I'm going to make a huge star."

When adults realize just how complicated this process is and how long it takes to develop these concepts, we're likely to become more relaxed, stop hurrying children, and have fun.

> Mara lives in Southern California. Her five-year-old grandson Abel lives nearby, and Mara helps out with child care when he's not in kindergarten. It's September and Abel's asthma has worsened because of the smoke from the nearby fires. His energy is low and he needs frequent rests. This is the second week he's home from school.
>
> Mara hears his frequent complaints. "I can't see my friends. It's boring!" She agrees and thinks of several games he enjoys. They play Go Fish and Crazy Eights, taking a break between games for Abel to use his inhaler and have a warm drink. Then Abel brings out his new set of dice and announces that he'll teach her to play his game. "I throw my dice. Then you throw your dice and you have to match my number. I played with my dad last night, and one time it took him 11 tries to match my number four. Ready, Grandma?"

Mara told this story as she talked about Abel's health. He and other children at his school often miss school because of their asthma. She always takes care of him and tries to find playful ways to involve and amuse him. She introduced Go Fish and Crazy Eights because he can play it while resting in bed. To play fast, he has to match the number of shapes on the card with the number on the card very quickly, without stopping to count up starting from one.

Mara said she enjoys his look of total concentration. She was also impressed with the dice game Abel showed her—and impressed too that her son, Abel's father, had remembered the simple dice game Mara used to play with him, including some that required adding and even easy multiplication.

Spatial Relationships

From birth, children learn about spatial relationships. They crawl under and over, and move objects toward and away from them. They see objects not in isolation but in relation to other objects.

For example, on this beautiful day, Romero and his grandchildren Tomás and Teresa are playing in their neighborhood park. The children roll down the grassy hill, then get up and beat their arms in the air as they run across the spacious field toward the playground equipment. They line up for a turn on the curvy slide. Then they climb up the pole and onto the small climber, then pull themselves up and over the top, and drop to the ground below. Consider all their bodily kinesthetic experiences of space!

Spatial relationships are basic to young children's everyday experiences, but we rarely talk about spatial relationships in our "mathematical conversations" with children. Children's books usually feature only regular shapes like triangles, circles, and squares, even though young children play with more complex shapes and construct many shapes themselves when they play with blocks and draw.

Yet many young children delight in learning long and difficult words like "estimating," "horizontal," and "octagon"—just as they might delight in telling you the names of dinosaurs. In fact, some shape names literally describe spatial relationships. The word "octagon," with its Greek origin *octagonās*, refers to eight-sided shapes. Think about the word "triangle" (tri-angle) and how the three sides of the triangle form three angles with one another.

So let's celebrate and encourage children's natural mathematical interests and skills. We can talk about the shapes they see in their own environments. Most objects children see every day aren't regular shapes like triangles, but irregular shapes like chairs, spoons, and bushes that are challenging to describe.

Children are also interested in their own bodies—and their bodies have irregular shapes. Some of my most vivid memories of play with my own children include times when we traced and cut out the body shapes of our family. This began when our daughter Alia was almost two. Derek and I would place a large piece of butcher paper on the floor so she could lie down on it. Then we'd use a marker to trace around her from head to toes. Forty-five years later, I can still picture her look of wonder when we cut it out and taped it on the wall so she could stand beside it. Sometimes Alia wanted to repeat this activity several times.

Months after Peter was born, we created our first family portrait—cut-outs of all four of us that Alia colored with crayons and that we taped to the wall. Over the years we followed with variations. Alia and Peter made cut-outs of their feet, hands, and shoes, as well as ours, and were awed seeing the dramatic contrasts of sizes and shapes.

As you might guess, we replayed this activity when our first grandchild Elijah was an infant. As I write this, Elijah is 19 years old, Zoë is 16, Ava is 7, and Jake is 3. I'd better get more rolls of paper and markers!

Patterns

What is a pattern and where do we see them? For example, Randell makes a pattern as he strings colored beads and repeats yellow, green, red, brown, yellow, green, red, brown, yellow, green, and so on. A pattern is a repeating regularity, like Randell's pattern of yellow, green, red, brown, We can find patterns every- where, in fabric designs, music, and poetry.

Young children's play with patterns is both fun for them and fun for grandparents to watch, whether we're there in person or watching virtually. Toddlers, preschoolers, and kindergartners delight in discovering and following patterns. They love to create patterns as they clap, drum, or whistle, hop and skip, draw pictures, or build with blocks.

Like all mathematical understanding, children's under- standing of patterns develops over time. At two, Aisha loved to copy her grandmother's simple pattern of claps. A year later, she could describe the pattern. "You clapped one time, then three, then over again."

Now, months later, Aisha creates and explains the pattern she made with Lego blocks. "First I put a red, then a blue, then a yellow, then a red, then a blue, then a yellow. Guess what I need next." The ability to recognize patterns is an important mathematical skill that children develop relatively early.

What patterns can you and your grandchild find in your own play? What about the way you and your grandchild set the table? Does your grandchild have clothes with repeating patterns? What patterns can you notice in the songs you sing? When you and your grandchild begin to see and play around with patterns, you'll soon discover them everywhere.

Mathematical Thinking Is Active Thinking

These stories show that mathematical thinking is active thinking. Opportunities arise all the time. As we play, we use key mathematical processes whether we are aware of them or not. This includes the ways that we problem solve, reason, speak with others, and record what happened with a photo or a drawing.

Young children think mathematically when they talk about what they're doing and their reasons for doing it. For example, this afternoon, Ayala and her grandparents are playing with blocks. Ayala asks, "This tower keeps falling down. What'll we do?" She is thoroughly engaged in this problem because it's her own, not merely a problem in a workbook.

She continues: "What block goes here?" "I'll try it this way. Do you have two short ones?" As she talks about what she's done, Ayala exclaims, "Look. It's standing! Grandma, let's take a photo."

The photo will be a record of what they did. In collaborative play, problems are joint challenges and so are the solutions—joyful and mathematical.

Ideas for Wandering Over the Mathematical Landscape

In deciding how and what to play, ask your grandchildren, "What will be fun today?" Stay in tune with your grandchildren's interests, to how and what they want to play. Maybe you'll play with blocks or paint, play in the sandbox, or play card games like Go Fish. These activities can help children develop number sense, spatial relationships, and patterns. Mathematics is everywhere.

Playing with Blocks

Many early childhood educators think that blocks are the ultimate materials for supporting mathematical reasoning. And we grandparents know that most young children love blocks.

Jenna is a passionate block builder. Since she was a toddler, she and her grandparents Diane and Barry have spent hours each week playing with Legos and Trio blocks. Recently, she received her cousins' collection of beautiful hardwood blocks. Even though they are called kindergarten or unit blocks, they can fascinate children for many years. The basic unit block is a square measuring 5½″ by 2¾″ by 1″. This set includes basic units, half units, and double units as well as small triangles, columns, and arches.

Today, Jenna and her grandparents are building castles with towers to stage their imaginative pretend play stories.

Jenna: "Should we build another tower on the castle over here so it's symmetrical? ... There're no more long blocks. I'll take these four short blocks ... I'm gonna put the second block here to balance the tower."

Diane: "Are there some more blocks there to finish the moat?"

Barry: "What about using these two half-circles for buttresses?"

As Diane's story shows, block play is fun and involves intellectual challenges for grandparents and grandchildren as they jointly solve problems.

Tips for Play with Blocks

Safety Note: Blocks designed for infants and toddlers should be large enough and shaped to be easily grasped and manipulated—just right for developing levels of hand-eye and motor coordination. They're safe because they're nontoxic and can be mouthed but not swallowed.

➢ Small cubes are just right for an older infant or toddler to grasp and sense the feel of a cube—a regular shape. When infants are about 12 months old, they might begin to move several blocks in what looks like an intentional way—perhaps stacking two blue blocks. Spontaneous play with simple blocks helps develop early number awareness because children see and handle small sets of two, three, or four

(cont.)

objects—combining, separating, and recombining them. Sixteen-month-old Ada experiences the feel of the smooth wooden blocks as she holds two in each hand. She tosses one away, and her grandmother Leni counts the remaining blocks aloud, "One, two, three ... Ada, where's the other block?" Leni retrieves the block and Ada tosses it again. A new game has begun—combining and separating a set of four blocks.

➢ A wide variety of blocks is available for children three years old and older. Small wooden blocks and blocks that connect are widely popular. These include blocks that stack, snap, link, or interlock. Some, like Lego and Trio blocks, are available in larger sizes for younger children and smaller sizes for older children. Other kinds of blocks come in different colors, shapes, sizes, and thicknesses. Children can use these to build and make patterns.

➢ Early childhood educators consider unit blocks the best type for developing mathematical reasoning. A set of wooden unit blocks will last forever, a family treasure to be shared and passed on to future generations—and to cousins like Jenna. Some blocks are twice the length, and others four times the length, of the basic unit. Sets include small and large triangles, ramp shapes, large and small cylinders, elliptical curves, quarter-circle arches, and half-circle buttresses.

➢ Homemade blocks are not only free but also fit the bill for introducing the novelty young children enjoy. Preschool and school-aged grandchildren and their grandparents appreciate the creativity of making homemade blocks, sawing and sanding wood, or making blocks from cardboard boxes.

Playful Young Mathematicians as Artists

Young children get both pleasure and understanding from art explorations that involve number sense, spatial relationships, and patterns. At just a year and a half old, Aiden moves energetically, drawing huge curved lines across the piece of paper with his large washable markers. Popular two-dimensional artful activities include drawing with water-based markers, crayons, colored pencils, and watercolors.

By the time they are older preschoolers or kindergartners, children's representational art takes new turns. Today, Matthew is carefully drawing a person standing next to a pine tree with a mountain in the background. He stops, looks up at his grandfather, considers the problem of perspective, and remarks, "I want to draw the mountain so it looks like it's really far away."

Three-dimensional art activities include playdough for toddlers and younger preschoolers and different types of clay for older children. Alla and Shasha's twin six-year-old grandchildren enjoy all kinds of modeling clay. This morning they're playing with their grandfather and creating imaginary animals. (See Chapter 9 for more art project ideas and resources.)

Playful Mathematics Outdoors

Opening the front door invites us to continue to wander over the mathematical landscape wherever we and our grandchildren live. We might go out the door across the field and down to the stream, or walk together to nearby shops or join friends playing in the sand area at the park. Consider these three scenarios in which Eli and Michael explore shapes, and Jenna sets herself a counting challenge.

Grandpa Dan and Eli, now five years old, are bundled up for their walk on this snowy day. Eli counts as they descend the front stairs. "Watch out. This third step is icy!" "The snow is up to the top of your boot, Grandpa." Passing a neighbor's yard, Grandpa asks, "What's that under the snow that's making that weird shape?" "I remember. It's that funny bush."

Three-year-old Michael and his great-grandmother Gloria walk to the store. They find a bench to take a break. While his great-grandmother rests, Michael collects small, flat pebbles and begins to build a shape in the dust beside the bench that he calls "my hut." He constructs the shelter by stacking the pebbles and covering the structure with a roof of leaves.

The cherries have begun to fall from the tree. Jenna announces, "I can pick two cherries at a time," and chants, "two, four, six, two, four, six ..."

Playing with Puzzles

Puzzles focus children's attention on shapes and spatial relationships, and on how individual shapes combine to form larger shapes and pictures. Puzzles with just a few pieces focus younger children's attention on the simple shapes of the pieces. Older preschoolers and kindergartners prefer more challenging puzzles with numerous irregularly shaped pieces that make complicated pictures. Grandparents who can't visit with their grandchildren in person find that puzzles make gifts that some children return to again and again, and they are a simple but lively activity to watch during virtual visits.

Tips for Puzzle Play

Enjoy creating your own activities and following your grandchild's interest. Stop while it's still fun and before your grandchild seems tired or frustrated.

➤ It's important that puzzles are not too difficult. A good puzzle for a child has enough pieces to be challenging but not frustrating.

➤ With a younger child, start by making a simple puzzle with two pieces. If a child can do this, make a three-piece puzzle. Simply cut one piece in two or make a different puzzle.

➤ It helps if the puzzle has a "frame" that shows the size of the finished puzzle, like the commercial puzzles for children. Children can also use the envelope of a greeting card— the puzzle pieces are the cut-up card—as a "frame" that shows the shape of the finished puzzle. This also solves the problem of keeping all the pieces together—simply put the pieces in the envelope and save for another time.

➤ Rather than buying commercial puzzles, you can create homemade ones by recycling materials like small cardboard boxes and greeting cards. Cut up the picture on the card into three or more pieces, depending on the skill of the puzzler. Your grandchildren can also enjoy creating puzzles for you to solve!

Grandparents and Grandchildren Together: Thinking Mathematically

Stories of grandchildren playing with their grandparents show that mathematics underpins so many activities. For young children, play is the primary means for developing mathematical understandings.

If play supports the development for all players, how might play support grandparents' mathematical understandings? In these stories, we see clear evidence of grandparents' appreciation of children's mathematical development.

What may be less obvious is that our own mathematical thinking is enhanced as we solve problems and answer the questions that naturally come up during play. "Grandpa, can you guess what pattern I made with these beads?" "Grandma, let's make this bridge longer."

Sometimes grandchildren ask the question or take the lead. Sometimes we do. As in all play, learning and discovery occur when all players are truly engaged. While our grandchildren discover, we grandparents can rediscover the beauty and joy of mathematics.

CHAPTER 9

Play, Creativity, and the Arts

An artful life trains the brain to work at finding alternatives and choices, solving problems and testing answers, and bypassing the known or accepted way of doing things to find new ways. An artful life will open the mind of a child and pave the way to become an adult who can think about and even create options—widely and wonderfully and joyfully! – Mary Ann Kohl (2019, p. xiii)

Visual Art

When Ba and Bapugi arrive, two-year-old Avi runs to the door with his box of crayons in hand. They told him that they'd bring some large construction paper. He hugs them, then leads them to the table, eager to start. Selecting green paper and a green crayon, he draws his picture by scribbling in large back-and-forth movements. The green lines he makes are distinct and bright because he can grip crayons more firmly now and press down harder. He points and says, "See, so fast ... go here ..." He continues to scribble while repeating, "And here, fast, so fast."

He stops and looks at his drawing with pleasure. Next, he chooses the bright red paper and scribbles faster back and forth, across and down. Then definitely finished, he turns, and looks up at his grandparents. "Look what a lot of drawing you did with your green crayon," Bapugi says. "If you're finished, I can write your name on your pictures." Avi nods and hands his pictures to his grandpa. His artwork completed, he's ready for a change of activity.

Avi looks forward to art activities, and so do his grandparents. It's exciting to see his interest and creativity blossom. Their weekly ritual of arriving with simple art materials inevitably sparks an excited reunion. It also seems to ease his transition from the joy of seeing his grandparents to his sometimes tearful separation from his mom who leaves for work and his sister to kindergarten. After his mom and sister leave, Avi settles down more easily when there's an engrossing art activity on offer. His concentration on his drawing soon deepens.

His grandparents often bring simple art materials to extend what Avi already has at home. Today it's a few pages of large construction paper, twice the usual size. Art activities are favorites for Avi and his sister Ria. Their mother introduced crayons and paper before their first birthdays and soon followed up with markers, chalk, and playdough.

Ba and Bapugi love watching and sometimes participating in their grandchildren's art explorations and discoveries. Creative art activities support Avi's desire for more independence. Today is a good example. He can select whatever color he likes, but his selection is limited to make his choices easier. He enjoys experimenting with crayons, markers, playdough, and tempera paints. He's learning some basic art techniques, like keeping water-colors vibrant by washing his brush in water each time before he switches colors. His grandparents also notice his push for independence when he puts on his art smock by himself and helps clean up.

The materials Avi's grandparents bring invite creative, open-ended art explorations—what art educators call *process art* that focuses on *doing* rather than making a product. Process art is playful art. Indeed, process art is inseparable from play.

There's a natural match between young children and open-ended process art. As in all playful activities, grandparents want their grandchildren to have freedom to choose, invent, explore, and discover. And, whether we're sitting across the table or visiting online, grandparents can rediscover art that is playful, even if we think we have no artistic talent. Time for process art, art that is open-ended and creative, is lively and fun at any age.

In *The Artful Parent,* Jean Van't Hul provides information and guidance that's useful to grandparents as well as parents:

> *The freedom to experiment and the encouragement to do so are especially important to the development of creativity. That's why I believe strongly in process-oriented art, which is about the open-ended exploration of materials and techniques. Because there is no right or wrong way to make art with this approach, it promotes flexible thinking, instills a willingness to take risks, and builds confidence. Children become confident in their creativity and problem-solving abilities, and they learn through experimentation and the observance of cause and effect. If I mix these two colors, what will be the result? If I sprinkle salt on the painting, how will it look? ... This is opposed to the overused practice of making art with an end result (often teacher imposed) in mind, which cuts off the potential for both creative exploration and whatever art or craft could have become. (Van't Hul, 2019, pp. 14–15)*

Realistic Expectations and Creative Possibilities

Understanding what children do at different ages guides our expectations and helps us discover a wider range of art materials and activities that our grandchildren might enjoy. We can see all aspects of our grandchildren's development reflected in their art.

What do your grandchildren like to do? How do they use art materials at different ages? What progress might you see over time?

Infants and Toddlers

Grandparents find it striking to see infants explore art materials with all their senses, just as they explore all materials. Give seven-month-old Kia a crayon and watch her examine it, smell it, push it, watch as it rolls, and—though we're teaching her not to—start to put it in her mouth. At 10 months, she makes faint marks on paper. What a discovery!

Soon infants become toddlers. In art, this is called "the scribble stage," though the word *scribble* doesn't acknowledge their accomplishments and joy. Toddlers draw lines, more lines, and then more lines in all directions across the page.

As their language develops, we sometimes hear toddlers talking to themselves about what they're doing, just as Avi did. Then, when children are about three years old, you might see them experimenting with curved lines. Some children may do this months later, but the progress of their drawings will usually be the same.

What other art materials do infants and toddlers enjoy? They want to explore *everything*, although they use all materials in their own way. Under your close supervision, and always with nontoxic materials, this is the perfect age to introduce different kinds of crayons, nonpermanent markers, chalk, and playdough. Watch Ella's grin as she pokes and squeezes playdough or uses fat chalk to make brilliant colors on a damp sidewalk.

Don't underestimate toddlers. With their growing strength and coordination, there's a wide world of media to explore! Grandparents find that with patient guidance toddlers can use a great variety of art media, including finger and tempera paints. Introduce tempera paints and watch their delight as they mix colors and create new ones (see the next section for tips on using art materials).

Most toddlers discover that "sticky" is so much fun. Some dive in immediately, relishing the feeling of sticky paste on their fingers and hands. Others hesitate, gingerly dabbing a paste stick on paper or experimenting with strips of masking tape or post-it notes that don't make their fingers so sticky. A favorite art activity for toddlers and their grandparents is making a collage on cardboard by pasting shapes of colored paper, photos from magazines, and torn strips of newspaper.

The Play Years

The play years are wondrous times for open-ended art. Three and four-year-old children infuse their boundless energy and imagination into their art, demonstrating that play and creative process art are inseparable.

We watch them go from scribbling straight lines to adding curved lines and spirals, and, within months, to closing spirals and coiled lines into irregular but definitely circle-like forms. Within about a year, circular forms sprout lines, and children announce they've drawn a person.

Grandparents take special delight in their grandchildren's drawings and paintings that have that distinctive, "classic" look of three and four-year-olds' art.

Soon after her third birthday, our granddaughter Zoë drew a person with stick arms and stick legs poking out of a large irregular circle. Her dog Charlie appeared as an irregular oval shape with four lines extending out. After a couple of months and many art experiences, her drawing of a person's head included two eyes, a nose and mouth, and two ears. Then, as is typical for most children, she began to draw an oval shape for the torso. Another smaller oval for the neck appeared in short order. Within months, the arms had hands and then fingers, and the legs had feet and then toes. And Charlie had a tail.

At this age children want their art to represent their world. With their increased fine motor coordination, longer attention spans, and increased use of symbols, they're beginning to draw whatever is important to them and to others around them. They show that their interest is social as they draw family and friends.

Some three and four-year-old grandchildren like to name what they draw or tell you a story about what's happening. Some will want you to write it down so everyone knows what it is, and they want to "read" it too. The amount of children's drawings can be massive. You may find it challenging to choose which ones to exhibit in the "gallery" on your refrigerator or bedroom wall and which ones to keep in your grandchild's art file.

Three and four-year-old children thrive when given opportunities to be more independent and to explore what they can do with a wider range of art materials—watercolors, different kinds of clay, a full palette of tempera paints, and a great variety of objects for collages. With their increased coordination, they enjoy tactile art techniques, whether they're rolling and coiling clay to make a bowl or using cotton swabs to make dotted designs with tempera paint.

Now they'll need more time and space for their art activities—particularly the more complicated, multistep projects they take on at this age, whether it's painting the clay horse they made last week or decorating a huge refrigerator box to use in their pretend play. Their growing social interests show up in small group art activities like painting a joint mural or making group collages from materials they've collected.

By about age four, children are learning to use simple representations and symbols in their open-ended art, perhaps adding a sun, a rainbow, a pine tree, and some numbers and letters. This signals their transition to the next stage, the art of older preschoolers and kindergartners.

Older Preschoolers and Kindergartners

Children's interest in art often evolves from process-oriented art to more product-oriented art. Now they want their drawings to look realistic, and they want you to recognize what they're drawing. "This is me next to my house." Grandparents may notice that children often develop a fixed set of steps they always use, whether it's to draw a person, an animal, or a house.

If you went to a kindergarten classroom, you might see that, although each child's drawings are different, they all have stereo-typed characteristics. A typical example is a picture of a house with one or two people and a tree next to it and, off to the side, a mountain and a sun above in the sky.

We understand their drawings better when we're aware that our grandchildren want to show that they're growing up and can draw realistic pictures like older kids do. Remember, too, that older preschool and kindergarten children show their desire for group membership by wanting to do things like their peers do. If we visit a classroom, we might see many children drawing similar pictures, perhaps skyscrapers one month and super-heroes the next.

In some ways, these products of children's art represent a big developmental step forward. But when we see them being less creative and spontaneous, it can seem like a big step backward. It's reassuring for us to remember that artistic development, like development in other areas, does not progress in a simple linear direction. Grandparents can step in and continue to offer inter-esting, engaging, and age-appropriate opportunities for their five and six-year-old grandchildren to engage in process art.

We know that by the time our grandchildren grow older and we think back on these first five years, we've often forgotten things that seemed absolutely unforgettable at the time. So much of what children do is fleeting and can't be saved, so it is especially wonderful to have photos and keep some of their early artistic efforts like drawings and paintings.

The Wonderful World of Art Materials for Young Children

Many of us remember the art materials we had when we were children and the fun of discovering new ones when our own children were young. These days, when we look for art materials for our grandchildren, it's become easier to find nontoxic, washable types.

On the other hand, the number of choices can seem overwhelming. It's reassuring to know that the basic categories are the same we remember from years gone by—crayons, pencils, markers, and chalks for drawing. Paints for painting. Clays for molding and sculpting. And anything a child chooses for making collages.

Crayons, pencils, chalk, and markers now come in many more shapes, sizes, and hues. You can help your grandchildren find the color they want by keeping them sorted by color and removing the outside paper from crayons. A newer type of marker is worth discovering—Kwik Stix are sticks of solid tempera paint in the form of markers. Children hold and draw with them like regular markers, but their drawings look like tempera paintings. Some grandparents who live far away mail art materials to their grandchildren and find that children like Kwik Stix because they are a novel surprise.

Sometimes, grandchildren want to bring out paints, but grandparents may hesitate. Painting may seem like such a messy activity. But try it yourself. Get into the spirit of process art and start painting. You might be surprised how satisfying it feels when you paint freely, without a goal in mind. Be brave. Try finger painting to music to awaken all your senses. And you can read the tips later in this section on how to protect clothes, floors, and furniture.

Today's grandchildren enjoy the same kinds of paints that children have enjoyed for more than a century. Introduce paints to your toddler, preschooler, or kindergartner and watch your grandchild's creative explorations. Small jars of tempera paints come in sets of bright colors and are sold widely. Always buy nontoxic and washable tempera paints for young children.

Start with a narrow brush and two colors. Help your younger grandchild practice rinsing the brush in water to keep the color bright before offering more colors. Grandparents can easily do what art teachers typically do—start with the primary colors of red, yellow, and blue before adding the secondary colors of orange, purple, and green. Then add white and black.

Watercolors are classic and always popular. Although younger children tend to "scrub" the paper, three and four-year-olds have the coordination to use a gentle touch. With tempera and watercolors, start with a single brush and then, perhaps, add a narrower one and wider one. Brushes with rubber grips made for children with physical disabilities are great for all younger children as well as grandparents with arthritis.

Doughs and clays delight the senses. Children who reach out to feel the texture of materials—the soft feel of velvet, the bumpy feel of corduroy, and the slippery feel of finger paints—are in their element when they can experiment with doughs and clays. Give your grandchildren considerable time to explore.

It's simple to make wonderful homemade playdough. Older preschoolers and kindergartners will enjoy making them with you. (See the Resources list at the end of this book for a link to Playdough Power, an article that includes recipes and numerous tips.) Children find baker's dough and some commercially sold clays special because they air dry so that children can keep and paint their artistic creations.

Early 20th century artists like Pablo Picasso and Georges Braque are famous for the multimedia artform of collage. Early childhood educators soon brought this creative, open-ended art form into the lives of young children, who then brought their creative treasures home to their families. The possibilities of collage are as expansive as our imaginations.

Some grandparents told me that they keep a box for collage materials, such as leftover construction paper, pieces of cardboard, cut-up postcards, gift cards, pages torn from magazines and newspapers, tissue paper, scraps of fabric, wallpaper, tape, colored yarn, and, of course, stickers. Children love to create bold three-dimensional collages, for example, by gluing small wood scraps to make a sculptural collage or adorning a shoebox with colorful objects.

Nature walks to find outdoor collage materials have long been a favorite with our grandchildren. They search for dried leaves, flower petals and seeds, and little sticks, berries, small acorns, and sometimes the dried shell of a roly-poly that the children place gently in their little basket.

Luca, now three years old, and Ada, six years old, head right for the art shelves when they visit Grandma Leni and Grandpa Hans. They know to take newspaper from the bottom of the pile and ask for help to cover the kitchen table. Then they choose from a collection of markers, watercolor pencils, rounded scissors, glue sticks, and collage materials. They are skilled at using these materials and cleaning up with minimal help.

Tips for Using Art Materials

- ➤ Familiarize yourself with art materials before offering them to your grandchild. Notice the appealing tactile as well as visual properties of many materials.

- ➤ Encourage children's interest by keeping the setup simple and present the new media and materials attractively, one at a time.

- ➤ Give children many opportunities to become confident using each material.

- ➤ Choosing materials:

  - » Safety: Select art materials for infants and toddlers that are nontoxic and washable. Pieces must be large enough so they can't be swallowed. Check to make sure scissors and other tools have rounded edges. Be alert to possible allergies to pigments, paste, glue, or other substances.

(cont.)

Tips for Using Art Materials (cont.)

- » Materials that are safe for infants and toddlers are good for all children. Before introducing new materials to preschoolers and kindergartners, consult with parents and review appropriate age recommendations. Remember that some materials make permanent stains.

- » Today's supermarkets and craft stores carry basic art materials. If you can, check art supply stores for specialty brands that artists choose. Specialty papers, crayons, and paints can make children's work more vibrant.

- ➢ Presenting materials:

  - » Keep the area organized and inviting so children can find materials themselves.

  - » For messy activities, protect tables with plastic tablecloths and cover the floor.

  - » Protect clothes: Some families turn old clothes into art clothes. Others prefer that children wear art smocks. Art smocks are easily made from an old adult shirt, or a plastic tablecloth or shower curtain. Children's art smocks can also be purchased.

  - » Keep a clean, damp cloth at hand to clean the area and wipe up spills, and another small damp cloth for children to wipe their hands. For paints, provide a small jar with clean water to rinse brushes.

- ➢ Teach children how to use tools.

  - » Check that scissors are the right size for your grandchild. Teach children how to hold scissors and carry them safely. Left-handed children's scissors are available.

  - » Help children learn to keep art tools and materials clean and in good condition. Help them learn to check that markers, tubes, and bottles of glue are capped, and paintbrushes are washed and stored bristles up.

- ➢ Make handwashing part of the cleanup routine.

Music

Elizabeth and David live in Toronto in the same house as their son Alex and his family. With five-year-old Pia and three-year-old twins, Mateo and Samuel, living upstairs, these grandparents always have lively stories to share. After-dinner music times have become a family ritual. Elizabeth and David had recently returned home from a trip to Vancouver when Pia invited them upstairs for "a concert." The children led their grandparents to specially arranged chairs. Then the three young performers stood up solemnly and Pia raised her baton. To their grandparents' great surprise, the children began a rousing rendition of O Canada, the Canadian national anthem, followed by Alouette sung in French.

Ying Yue video chats with her niece Betty every weekend and always looks forward to a special time with Mason, her four-year-old grandnephew. On this day, Ying Yue claps her hands as Mason beats out a rhythm on his bongo drum. This afternoon, they're accompanied by the album *Latin Playground* recorded by Putumayo Kids. Ying Yue says she doesn't think of herself as particularly musical. She's never played an instrument or sung in a choir. But she's always enjoyed a wide range of music and started a playlist of baby songs before Mason was born. Since then, she's compiled several playlists they both enjoy that include their favorite singers, classical music, and popular children's songs in several languages. She's thrilled that Mason often asks to make music together during their video chats.

These stories show how music can be part of young children's everyday lives and point to the rich musical traditions across family backgrounds, culture, and language. When we incorporate songs and instruments in play with our grandchildren, we give them free rein to express themselves more fully.

When thinking about music for infants and toddlers, we might think first of singing lullabies. But even newborns hear a great range of music, whether it's an older brother singing, an aunt streaming a favorite instrumental, or even background music from a television commercial. Traditional baby games and songs are wonderful introductions to differences in melodies, rhythm, tempo, pitch, and tonal quality.

Many babies babble rhythmically. Even before saying their first words, we hear them making melodic tonal sounds. When our grandchildren were infants, Derek would sing Old MacDonald's Farm, ending each stanza with the rousing refrain "E-I-E-I-O!" Sometimes the baby would echo "EEEEE" and hold the note for several beats just like Grandpa did.

Popular songs for toddlers and preschoolers often follow a similar pattern with their catchy words and repeating phrases. Some have a call-and-response format, like the traditional Alouette (French-Canadian), Did You Feed My Cow (U.S.), Vamos a la Mar (Guatemalan), and recent popular children's songs like Boom Chicka Boom.

Rhythm instruments are favorites with children around the world. Grandparents love to watch toddlers moving their bodies to the rhythm and clapping their hands. Spoons, baby rattles, pots and pans, maracas, and simple wooden drums are great rhythm instruments for toddlers as well as their older siblings. Preschoolers and kindergartners have great success with xylophones, paddle drums, bells, bongo drums, kalimbas, and tambourines.

Whatever their age and experience, it's fun for grand-children and grandparents to pick up rhythm instruments and instantly beat out their own rhythms or accompany their favorite musicians by clapping, marching, or stomping their feet.

Three to five-year-olds like to expand their repertoire with the wider range of tone and rhythms they can make with various instruments, from whistles, kazoos, and recorders to pianos and ukuleles (ukuleles are a better choice than guitars because of their smaller size and four rather than six strings). Children and grand-parents delight in including family names in a familiar song, and even making up totally new verses. With their far-ranging imagi-nation and growing sense of humor, young children can have fun making up their own songs.

Homemade instruments help children and grandparents create their own music while learning more about tone, pitch, and rhythm. It's fun and easy to make a tambourine from paper plates or a guitar from a tissue box and rubber bands. Drums with varying tones can be made from a round oatmeal box or a coffee can for softer drumming indoors. A hubcap or a large metal can may be used for loud, bold drumming outdoors.

Listening to different kinds of music broadens children's creative musical palette. There's a universe of music grandchildren can explore, from traditional music from around the world to classical music, and from rock to opera. Grandparents can select from hundreds of musical recordings for young children available on CDs or for streaming online:

- Connect generations by introducing your grandchildren to favorites you remember from your own childhood as well as music their parents remember from theirs.

- Check out compilations produced by Putumayo Kids, such as *American Playground*, *African Playground*, *Latin Playground*, and *Asian Dreamland*.

- Introduce beloved singers of young children's music such as Woody Guthrie, Ella Jenkins, José-Luis Orozco, Raffi, and Sonia De Los Santos.

- Seek out recording artists, like Greg & Steve, whose songs are designed to encourage movement.

- Ask your local children's librarian for recommendations.

Extend musical experiences with books that illustrate well-known songs as well as books about types of music and famous musicians. Sing along with the many books based on songs such as:

- *There Was an Old Lady Who Swallowed a Fly* by Simms Taback

- *Little Chickies/Los Pollitos* by Susie Jaramillo

- *A Tisket, a Tasket* by Ella Fitzgerald (as illustrated by Ora Eitan)

- *Hush! A Thai Lullaby* by Minfong Ho

- *Every Little Thing* by Bob Marley and Cedella Marley

Kindergartners enjoy books about famous musicians such as *Dizzy* by Jonah Winter and *Before John Was a Jazz Giant* by Carole Boston Weatherford.

Four, five, and six are perfect years for a young child to attend a live performance with a grandparent. Prepare your grandchild for this new experience to help ensure a richer, more positive experience for all. Many communities have performances appropriate for young children, ranging from musicians playing children's songs to high school concerts to more formal musical events.

As we saw with Elizabeth and David's grandchildren, being part of spontaneous musical ensembles gives young children the joy of being part of a group. A gathering in a park or a family outing are perfect times for young children to feel part of the group—they can simply join the chorus of old favorites like If You're Happy and You Know It, Clap Your Hands or

De Colores. Playful music connects generations and enlivens our relationships.

Movement

Our mother encouraged my sister and me to be creative and love art, music, and movement. Looking back, I particularly admire her for dancing with us. This wasn't easy. She had polio as an infant and was unable to walk as a child until she'd had many operations. When my sister Leni and I were little, she wore a brace and had difficulty walking.

But she loved moving to music. I picture her dancing with us—holding onto a chair for balance and swaying to classical music or sitting and shimmying to a favorite jazz piece. With her bright eyes and dazzling smile, she'd encourage us to dance. Leni and I did. And we still do.

Children love moving, especially moving to music by themselves and in synchrony with others. Watch a grandfather hold a baby gently while singing and dancing, or see a grand-mother smile as a toddler bounces energetically in time to music.

Creative movement is powerful. Infants sway and bounce to the rhythm. Toddlers try to turn around and jump along with the older kids. Preschoolers and kindergartners often hum or sing aloud as they leap around the yard or dance to a favorite tune.

Children's movement links their experiences—real and pretend—and lets their creativity soar. Through movement and dance, children develop a sense of themselves and their bodies, and improve their stamina, coordination, balance, and strength.

Numerous opportunities for creative movement are especially important during the early years when children can't express themselves verbally. They express their emotions with their whole bodies—happy, sad, excited, curious. As they sway, leap, wiggle, and bounce, they express themselves kinesthetically through their bodies.

Preschool children love *big* movements like galloping, hopping, turning, and jumping—but also tiny gentle movements like tiptoeing or gliding softly. Watch them move like their favorite animals. They can parade as a huge elephant lumbering on the savanna, or run swiftly like a gazelle, or so very slowly like a sloth moving across a branch.

Grandparents have always promoted young children's movement in many ways, from providing homemade rhythm instruments so grandchildren can create their own movements, to introducing easy circle dances that grandparents remember from childhood.

We know young children have fun with accessories that cue for movement. Children love to move so their capes, scarves, and ribbons float and swirl. Their stuffed animals, puppets, or masks of animal faces can inspire them to move quickly like a deer, slowly like a turtle, or majestically like an elephant. Of course, toddlers, preschoolers, and kindergartners experience particular fun leading their grandparents around the mulberry bush and falling down, or dancing to songs as they sing together.

Is this creative movement or dance? Connie Bergstein Dow explains, "Creative movement is an art form whose medium is the human body in motion. The four basic elements of dance are the body and its range of motion, space, time, and energy" (2015, p. 40).

Look at how children explore range of motion, space, time and energy:

- Children explore their body's range of motion as they extend their arms and legs as widely as they can, curl into the tiniest ball, or twist to make a pretzel.

- They explore space as they make believe they're snakes slithering around the couch and through the chair legs, or dance with their siblings, trying not to bump into each other.

- They explore time as they make different patterns as they move—two slow steps, then three quick ones, two slow steps, then three quick ones.

- They explore energy creatively as they march quickly with high steps to the fast rat-a-tat of a drum, then slow down as the rhythm slows. And, finally ... Stop!

And, of course, young children have great fun exploring the social aspects of music as they move with other children—and their grandparents!

It's helpful to remember that after such energetic activities, most young children need some transition to help quiet down. Transitions can take the form of slowing down with several gentle yoga poses, singing a quiet song, or reading a book together.

Movement activities to slow down not only make wonderful transitions but also help children learn ways to use their imagination to calm themselves. "Pretend you're a leaf gently falling down, down, down to the ground." "Pretend you're a large, heavy ball slowly, slowly rolling to a stop."

Celebrating Play, Creativity, and the Arts

Both children and adults flourish when they have enough time to play together and follow their interests in art, music, and movement. We grandparents delight in our grandchildren's creative artistic endeavors. Some of us joke that our refrigerators have become large frames for our grandchildren's drawings. Many of us who are unable to visit the children we love in person find that music and movement help us feel more in sync and connected with our grandchildren during virtual visits.

We love to share stories and videos of grandchildren singing, drumming, dancing to music, drawing, and painting. But most of all, we love time with our grandchildren, feeling inspired, and participating in an artful life widely, wonderfully, and joyfully!

THE GIFT OF PLAY

CHAPTER 10

The Gift of Play
Continues
Enhancing Close,
Joyful Relationships
Throughout the Years

As much as we enjoy playing with our grandchildren when they are young, we also look forward to the years ahead. It seems easier to play with grandchildren who are more independent and don't need constant supervision. At the same time, it can be challenging when older grandchildren develop their own interests and spend more time with friends. Whatever their age, we want to have close relationships with our grandchildren and want them to know that we love them. Close, joyful relationships develop over time. What is the role of play in these relationships?

In Chapter 2, I talked about how play promotes close, loving relationships with young children. Recall how Dr. Julie Nicholson conveyed the special role of play as allowing grandparents to express love through words and gestures that communicate, "you are a gift to me and to us." And, as Dr. Mary Sickles explained:

> *You're sharing an emotional moment. You're communicating your affection and sharing pleasure. It's genuine communication, genuine pleasure. You're aligning your emotions. You're feeling you're on the same wavelength— super-connected.*

The takeaway points from that chapter are the same no matter the age of our grandchildren.

- Play has the power to enhance close and loving relation-ships. Play is about having fun together and delighting in one another. As one grandparent said, "When you play, showing affection is part of the package."

  The favorite activities that you and your grandchildren ⌐th enjoy are ones where your interest and theirs meet.

- The magic of one-on-one time is often found in simple one-on-one experiences. Show your love by being flexible and responsive. Relaxed pleasurable times lead to deeper conversations.

Playful Times from Middle Childhood Through Young Adulthood

I think it's helpful for grandparents to know that older children think about play differently. By the time they start elementary school, they want to consider themselves older kids and begin to think of play as something little kids do. Typically, they use "play" in the more restrictive sense, the way they hear older children and adolescents talk about play. Even though they still talk about "playing basketball" or "playing a guitar," they talk about activities they used to call "play" as things they "like" or "do for fun."

Although older grandchildren may not talk about "playing" with their grandparents, they still talk about the fun they have with us. Myriad playful activities remain at the heart of relationships with their grandparents.

Enjoying Playful Times Throughout the Elementary School Years

During the middle childhood years, grandparents find a host of ways to have fun together. Some are new while others are continuations of favorite activities from when children were younger—whether it's reading books, making up stories, playing ball, cooking, creating art or music, taking walks, doing puzzles, playing board games, cycling, or watching movies together.

Just because children are older, activities don't have to be more complicated. For example, when my grandchildren were preschoolers, they loved telling jokes and riddles. Their sense of humor grew as they did. After they started reading, they discovered books of jokes and riddles and loved telling jokes that made us laugh or riddles that kept us guessing. Ava asks, "Why didn't the dog play ball?" We guess twice, and then she tells us the answer, "Because it was a boxer."

Steve and Linda talk about the fun they have baking with their grandchildren. One grand tradition is making big batches of their annual holiday cookies. It began when their grandchildren were little, with grandparents doing most of the work. Now their grandchildren do most of the work while Steve and Linda watch appreciatively. It's fun for everyone to eat cookies and talk as they wait for the next batch to come out of the oven.

Baking illustrates plainly how children become more skillful and independent during middle childhood. It's exciting for grandparents to notice that their grandchildren are not only growing taller and stronger but also developing the coordination and the agility they need, for example, to pour and measure ingredients.

During the middle school years, development becomes more gradual. However, we know that there's a big difference between the first grader who shows us her missing front tooth and the sixth grader who proudly models her graduation dress.

My 11-year-old granddaughter Leah is quite outgoing.
She laughs easily, even at my dopey jokes. We like to draw

together, play cards, and just kid around. Now that she's older, I talk with her about her schoolwork and the books she's reading. She has a great sense of humor and loves Shel Silverstein's books of amusing poems.

Dr. Rebecca Wheat, a longtime educator and author, talks about what she's learned from her own experience as a grandparent:

It's all about following the child's lead. See what the child is interested in. At different ages, there are so many different opportunities.

She also talks about two of her own grandchildren, Lola and Tayo.

Lola is nine. She's in a singing group that gives concerts and loves playing basketball. Her brother Tayo is 13. He plays the saxophone in the school band and also plays basketball. I'm always eager to join the family going to their concerts and basketball games. Because I know they're interested in music, sports, and science, I try to think of nearby opportunities. I'll say, "Let's all go to The Nutcracker," *or "Let's go to the Academy of Science."*

Many grandparents talked about attending a grandchild's special events, such as sports, plays, concerts, and open houses. These events provide a special window into their grandchild's interests and accomplishments, and often lead to good conversations. Some grandparents who live far away spoke about planning their visits around these special times.

We know that grandchildren's changing interests often mirror their growing abilities. Children need to be able to think strategically when they play more complicated card games or play sports like soccer. The expertise needed for physical activities also reflects the child's development. For example, many craft projects call for greater fine muscle coordination while running and swimming involve greater large muscle strength and coordination.

Derek and I have many memories of family times at the beach. Often, the kids would ask him to "play the game." First, they'd all race down to the water as the waves receded. Then they'd scamper up quickly to avoid the water as the waves rolled back because, otherwise, they would turn into frogs!

Every grandparent I spoke with talked about memorable trips with grandchildren in elementary school, whether it was a simple day trip, a longer vacation with the whole family, or a week-long stay at the grandparents' house.

Every summer since they were young, Olivia (12 years) and Ayanna (11 years) spend a week with their grandparents in upstate New York. Though each visit is different, Shelley and Mike know there are certain favorites the girls look forward to repeating, including riding the classic antique carousel or going to the Strong National Museum of Play and baseball games. Now that the girls are older, Shelley and Mike let them ride their bikes around the neighborhood.

During the COVID-19 pandemic, the girls had to stay at home. All of them missed their yearly visit and talked about ways to maintain their connection. Since Olivia and Ayanna had become engrossed in reading the newspaper each day, Shelley and Mike suggested they write a family newsletter.

For several weeks, Olivia and Ayanna conducted interviews and wrote stories about their lives, friends, and relatives. Their grandparents thought several pieces were particularly well done, such as a story about the protests against racial violence and their artistic renderings of people wearing masks. They typed their stories, drew illustrations, and took photos. They and their grandmother Shelley had almost daily virtual discussions to talk about their progress. After a while, Shelley realized that their interest had waned, and they became absorbed in other activities.

As this story shows, middle childhood is a time when grand-parents can help grandchildren learn more grown-up skills in a relaxed way. I heard grandparents talk about helping a grandchild learn computer skills, play sports, and use more complicated electric appliances like a sewing machine and an electric drill. Some grandparents are able to pass on special skills or knowledge that can become a delight for older children, from using a potter's wheel to their love of traditional music.

The reverse is also true. Our grandchildren delight in demon-strating their growing expertise by teaching us something new, whether it's tips on using a smartphone or how to play their favorite game. One grandfather recalled the afternoon his grandson taught him to play the Nintendo game *Mario Kart*. Another talked about hiking and how his grandchildren taught him the uses of various plants they saw and how to identify animal tracks.

Of course, grandparents know that children often want to spend more time with friends as they get older. "I'm still as eager as ever to make special times for favorite activities with my grandchildren. Being with them and their friends is less than I desire, but because I want to be with them, I do it without complaining—and feel lucky."

Grandparents crave special times for relaxed, informal conversations. These are moments when they feel particularly close to their grandchildren. Longer, leisurely trips are special, but even short times together can lead to long conversations, whether it's a hike along the creek, going out for an ice cream treat, or dancing to music. Derek or I are always ready to join Elijah or Zoë when they take their dog Charlie for a walk. Whether we talk much or not, we love this relaxed time for companionship.

Steve laughed recalling a five-hour marathon game of Monopoly with his grandson Will. These hours gave them lots of time to have long, unplanned conversations. He offers this advice:

THE GIFT OF PLAY

*Grandparents can give their grandchildren the gift of time—
and let them play to their hearts' content. We know that
it's hard for parents to do this because they're so busy. As
grandparents, we have the time.*

By the end of middle childhood, our role as grandparents has changed dramatically. Families no longer need our help with the tasks of child care. We feel fortunate when these older grandchildren still enjoy doing things together.

These are the years when grandchildren take part in more adult family activities, whether it's cooking, harmonizing to family songs, or participating in the more adult games their family plays. Several grandparents told me of the pleasure they take in introducing a family game they learned as children, such as cribbage, Gomoku, or Yahtzee.

Our grandchildren are growing up. These are the years when grandparents can look at their grandchild and catch a glimmer of what that child might be like in the years ahead.

Enjoying Playful Times During Adolescence

When my grandchildren were very young, I'd hear friends talk about the great times and wonderful adventures they were having with their teenage grandchildren. Now that my older grandchildren are 16 and 19, I agree wholeheartedly.

Doesn't this contradict what we hear about adolescent development? This is certainly not the picture of adolescence we get from popular media!

Research shows that most adolescents experience ups and downs. For some, adolescence is more difficult and, for others, a smoother ride. So much happens during a relatively short time.

Adolescents are going through puberty, thinking more about their social life, and facing the pressures of demanding classes and more homework. Many spend many hours contemplating their identity, their hopes, worries, and dreams for their future.

When we consider all this, we're less apt to take some of their behaviors personally and can be more supportive. We aspire to be nonjudgmental listeners and want our adolescent grandchildren to feel comfortable with us. We want to have many good times together.

This book is about play and about how having fun together strengthens relationships. This is certainly true during adolescence. Whether our grandchildren are going through a smoother or more difficult time, we want them to know we love them and want to be with them.

Consider Dr. Rebecca Wheat's advice again, "It's all about following the child's lead. See what the child is interested in." What does this mean when our grandchildren are adolescents?

"Following their lead" means being sensitive to grandchildren's moods and feelings. Adolescents don't want to be treated like young children. We follow their lead when we're respectful of their desires, including whether to be alone or with a friend. Everyone is happier when we change our grandparenting to be in tune with our grandchildren.

Adolescents want us to acknowledge that we know they're growing up. At any age, it's important to follow grandchildren's interests. Grandparents talked about times spent together cooking meals, listening to music or singing and playing instruments, playing more sophisticated games, going to favorite restaurants, and camping with adolescent grandchildren and their family.

Grandparents would also suggest an activity or experience in line with their grandchild's interests, including going to the theater, visiting a bird sanctuary, and watching them at a skateboard park. During the COVID-19 pandemic, one grandmother and her granddaughter took a virtual yoga class together.

Everyday and special activities can support adolescents' growing sense of themselves as capable and knowledgeable. I like the following example because it shows what can happen when grandparents step back and let a teenager take responsibility:

When we planned a family vacation in Oregon with our son's family, our granddaughter Hana volunteered to research places to stay. She came up with the awesome idea of staying at The Tiny House Hotel in Portland, Oregon. Everyone had a great time. We learned a lot about tiny houses and the tiny house movement.

One grandmother described a kayak trip with her two teenage granddaughters, recalling the time together as "the golden hours." Her granddaughters are cousins who live in different states and rarely see each other. As the three floated lazily down the river, the girls serenaded their grandmother and shared openly about their lives, vastly different experiences, and dreams for the future.

At this age, relationships between grandchildren and grandparents become more of an exchange of conversation and activities. As children mature, they begin to see their grandparents as adults with personalities, interests, skills, strengths, and weaknesses. They want to hear more about your history and what you believe.

Grandchildren now enjoy doing things that are fun for their grandparents—not simply because the grandchildren are more capable, but because they love their grandparents and want to delight them.

Barry and his two granddaughters have always had close relationships. Jenna is now a teenager with a busy social life, but she knows that she and her grandpa have a great time together whatever they do.

Jenna came over the other day to work in the garden since I can't do that anymore. I sat up on the deck while she weeded. It's a big garden. Lots of weeds. I told her I'd pay her since she's saving for clothes. While she worked, we joked around and laughed just as we always do. Jenna worked for six hours, but she stopped me when I went to pay her. "Grandpa, I think we fooled around for at least two hours, so just pay me for four."

Every grandparent I spoke to had personal experiences of times when a teenager was having difficulties or seemed less engaged with the family. The advice to know our grandchild's interests and follow their lead is especially helpful during these times.

We live a thousand miles away from two of our grandchildren and usually see them only a few times a year. Recently, our 15-year-old grandson has seemed more uninvolved when we visit. He'll spend a little time with us when we first arrive, but then stays in his room or goes to a friend's house. Just before we arrived, his parents gave him an old car to fix up. He was busy working on that car most of the time we were there. I don't know anything about fixing cars, but I know it's his passion.

I asked if I could watch and he agreed. I stood around for about 20 minutes before I asked him to tell me what he was doing. He really perked up and explained what the problem was and what he was doing. He talked more to me than he had all week. I was impressed—and told him so—with how much he knew and that he explained everything so clearly. For the rest of the visit, I spent a lot of time watching him work on his car and felt much more connected.

As grandchildren get older, so do we grandparents—and that presents other challenges. Our active participation in some activities decreases as we grow older and more physically limited while our grandchildren are growing stronger, faster, and more proficient.

Personally, I know I'm walking more slowly. When our family goes hiking, I'm glad I can count on one of our grandchildren to slow down to keep me company. Similarly, Derek pointed out, "Now that I'm older, I tend to watch and talk with them more about soccer and basketball rather than playing with them like I used to do."

Technology is one area in which many adolescents have more expertise than we do. Those of us who no longer drive or live far from our grandchildren turn to technology to feel connected. Derek and I do the same, although we live only an hour away from our teenage grandchildren.

Our grandchildren have taught us to stay in touch more often with a short text or emoji. When it's not a good time for a virtual visit, we love receiving a one-line text from them like "Enjoy your dinner" or "I love you, Grandpa" or "Good night, Grandma" or simply a smiling emoji.

Adolescents are old enough to appreciate how special four generations in the family can be. Whenever Gamma Essie's great-grandchildren call to say they're coming, she knows they'll always ask for her chocolate chip cookies. And, just as she did when they were younger, Essie brings out the old family photo albums, which inevitably leads her to tell tales of family history while her great-grandchildren listen with rapt attention.

Looking Forward to Playful Times During Young Adulthood

Young adulthood refers to the years from about 18 to 25, the years from high school graduation through training, first jobs, or college. A growing number of psychologists describe this period as "emerging adulthood."

Most of these young people are more independent yet don't have the work and family responsibilities of adults. To them, the future seems open. So many possibilities exist. Emerging adulthood is when many young people feel free to explore—it's a time to try different paths in their social lives, work, and world view without the commitment expected of adults.

I've noticed that when I use the term "emerging adulthood," people are quick to understand that it emphasizes the process of "emerging," rather than simply the end goal of "adulthood." More important, I find that "emerging adulthood" resonates with the emerging adults themselves as a helpful way of thinking about their own development. I ask my grandson Elijah how it feels to be 19 and he explains:

I feel different from when I was in high school. I'm in college and out of my home environment, but I still relate to my high school experiences and how I thought and felt. And I don't feel that I'm fully an adult yet. When circumstances are right, I feel more adult. It's different when I come home and I'm with my high school friends. There's an expectation you'll fall into old habits. There's an emphasis on falling into either role, to go back and forth depending on what's called for. It's less to do with the people I'm with but more with the physical place, the location. I haven't seen my friends much

at all during the pandemic, and I still have fallen into old
habits.

I asked Elijah what he likes doing with his grandparents now that he's in college:

I enjoy just hanging out together and chatting about
whatever, like how I hang out with my friends. I like doing
regular family things and cooking meals or going out for
dinner and talking about food. That never gets old. When
I'm with you, I like talking about my college stuff. College is
something we've both experienced. I just like hanging out
and seeing you and Grandpa and my Dutch grandparents,
Oma and Opa. There's always an excitement regardless of
when I've talked to them.

Reilly is 20 and lives with her mother and grandmother in a rural area. She's a sophomore in college and currently takes courses online. Reilly talks at length about the great times she has with her grandmother:

We always spent hours together drawing, painting, taking
long walks, and making photo albums. I'm teaching my
grandmother how to use technology to make music playlists,
and I answer the questions she has about her smartphone
and computer.

Steve and Linda give a grandparents' perspective when they talk about how they keep in contact with their 22-year-old grandson who lives in another state.

Nick has always been an outdoor person who likes
challenges and being independent. Since graduating from

THE GIFT OF PLAY

high school, he's worked as a lineman for an electric
company in Wyoming. It's an outside job that offers the
challenges and independence he loves. We know that we
need to be the ones to reach out. When we call, it's generally
a time to catch up and we always talk about his job.

Joyful Memories: Looking Back on Early Childhood

We grandparents have many memories of playing with our grandchildren when they were little. What memories do our grandchildren have when they get older? Do they have memories of playing with us when they were little—building castles with blocks, racing cars around the living room, splashing in puddles on rainy days, or reading their favorite books over and over? In this section, I'll talk about grandchildren's point of view—when grandchildren look back on their early memories of being with their grandparents, what do they remember? What did they enjoy?

My curiosity led me to ask my two older grandchildren, Elijah and Zoë, what memories they had of being with their grandparents when they were young. Some answers were more predictable. Some were surprising. Elijah and Zoë told me spontaneously how much they enjoyed talking about what they remembered.

I quickly learned that when I slowed my pace, young people had time to remember more and time to enjoy their memories— and so did I. I had hurried along during my conversation with

Elijah. I slowed down when I spoke with Zoë and waited so she could recall something more.

Zoë started out by telling me that she didn't remember much, but then one memory led to another. Soon she was happily engrossed and amazed at all she recalled. This is a shortened version of her response:

A favorite memory is going to the beach with you, Grandpa, and Elijah. We'd run away from the waves and pretend that if they touched you, you'd turn into a frog.

Whenever Elijah and I would stay the night at your house, we'd get up really early and drink hot chocolate. Grandpa would read us the books from the Redwall series and did the voices of all the characters. One time I slept over and woke up in the night and missed my parents and started freaking out. You got up and read to me and I felt better.

I loved going to the Lawrence Hall of Science and spending lots of time building with the KEVA blocks. I loved the holidays, and a lot of my memories revolve around food. I remember all of us sitting around the table and how we'd end up laughing super hard.

My Oma and Opa visit us almost every year and stay for about a month. When I was little, I'd go upstairs to see them as soon as I got up and they always had a treat from Holland waiting for me. My Oma is a great cook and she makes delicious omaletje. They'd always go to the store to buy lots of cheese and things to cook Dutch foods.

I remember sitting side by side with my Opa in the living room and playing video games like golf on his tablet. In the evenings we'd sit around laughing together, and eating

Oma's wonderful food, especially laagje om laagje, *and hearing Oma and Opa talk about our relatives in Holland.*

If you'd like to try a conversation like this with your grand-child, you needn't talk only about their earliest memories. Do what you both enjoy. By slowing down, both of you will have more time to enjoy their memories. If you're hesitant, these prompts may start the conversation rolling: What memories do you have of having fun together when you were little? What other memories do you have from when you were little?

My conversations with Elijah and Zoë led me to speak with other teenagers and young adults. Many were grandchildren of friends and relatives. Several grandchildren and grandparents spoke with their friends and relatives. These are snippets from other grandchildren's conversations:

I remember getting picked up from kindergarten. There was often a surprise in the car seat like a snack or a little toy. I also remember making art and doing ceramics. I remember roughhousing, especially fake wrestling with my grandpa.

I remember when we picked out Maury, our cockapoo. I loved it when we went to the bakery before school and bought cookies for the teachers. I loved so much what we did together.

When I was little, my sister and I would make big Lego towers with our grandparents. We drew, painted, and played dress up with our grandma's hats. I remember sleeping over at my other grandparents' house. We woke up and the dogs were there, but our grandparents were gone, so we went to look for them and they were making waffles with ice cream.

My grandpa took care of me a lot since my mom worked weekends. I had a train set and a track the trains went around. We'd play engineers and conductors and take long trips. I remember that we'd read together and take long walks. Whenever it started snowing, Grandpa always wanted to go outside and play in the snow. Even when it was slushy, we'd walk the few blocks to the bakery and share a peanut butter cookie.

Most adolescents and young adults recalled the fun of doing something that seemed very special. It might be the time they sat on the front stoop to watch a big parade with floats passing by, or stayed overnight at their grandmother's house and got up before dawn to watch the sunrise together, or took a family trip to visit a grandparent who lived abroad.

Most typically, their memories were of the fun they had doing more ordinary things, like playing in the park, having meals with their grandparents and other family members, riding their trike, taking neighborhood walks, doing puzzles together, drawing with colorful markers, or video chatting every week and listening to a grandparent read a book.

Do you notice that the memories grandchildren recall are the same kinds of playful activities that grandparents like to share when they talk about playing with young grandchildren?

Although every grandparent I spoke with had treasured memories of playing with their grandchild when they were infants and toddlers, most of the vivid memories these young people recalled happened when they were four or five years old. What's the explanation?

Child development research shows that few of us have any memories from before we were about three years old. One possible explanation is that the brain has not developed well enough to store memories for a long time. A second, related explanation is that children's ability to speak is limited until they're about three. So, the experiences that occur before that age are not remembered as "stories" of what they did. Whatever the reasons, although many two and three-year-old children can be very talkative, these memories are apt to fade over time.

I think this is one reason older children, adolescents, and young adults like hearing stories about themselves as young children as well as stories that convey family connections and affection. The important point is that, whether or not they recall memories from their early years, grandchildren can have great fun seeing photos and hearing others tell stories. This is a cue for us to tell stories, share stories as a family, and take out our photos.

I love hearing Corann tell stories about her family's lively gatherings. Her children and grandchildren always ask her to cook traditional family dishes, like Liberian rice and spinach stew with salmon and beef or chicken and rice. Corann laughs and tells me, "Food loosens the tongues, and everyone becomes merrier." Conversations flow and her grandchildren join the laughter as her four children recount story after story from their childhood.

> *Practically every time we get together since my husband Abraham passed away, my eldest son Deb recalls memories about his father that show how much he loved his parental role. These are sometimes humorous, and we all laugh. Even the younger grandchildren enjoy memories of their grandfather. It means a lot to me that my grandchildren love to spend their time together as a family.*

In Anne and Mike's family, sharing photos together has long been a favorite activity. Anne explains:

> *We want to create warm and loving memories. Memories that hopefully will last for both grandkids and grandparents. One thing that always stands out is Mike's love of taking photos for all occasions. It's great when our family is together, going through the photos and talking. These days, even though most of us like taking photos on our phones, we still print out many of Mike's photos. This gives everyone something tangible to hold on to and not get lost in the cloud!*

Grandchildren's fond memories are a tribute to the importance of play in their lives as young children. Their memories celebrate play at the very heart of grandparent and grandchild relationships. Sharing joyful stories with family members not only creates new memories but also brings us close together as a family.

THE GIFT OF PLAY

Celebrating Play in the Lives of Grandparents and Grandchildren

Grandchildren's memories are a tribute to the importance of play at the heart of grandparent and grandchild relationships. Play connects generations. Play enriches our grandchildren's lives and our own.

So many grandparents revel in stories and conversations about playing with their grandchildren. Grandparents' stories, the research on play, and conversations with experts in the field underscore the multiple benefits of play for older adults and young children. Play is essential for grandchildren and grandparents—and playing together magnifies its power.

Throughout *The Gift of Play* I have highlighted the special role of grandparents. By shining a light on play, I hope that I have shown how we can create more opportunities for play that engage and delight our grandchildren.

Each of the chapters focused on different aspects of play. The first chapters described the importance of play and showed how play enhances loving relationships. From birth and throughout the first five years, play together deepens our relationships.

Chapters 4 through 9 explored different dimensions of play, from language to pretend play, outdoor play, science, mathematics, and the arts. When we look at each topic more deeply, we can appreciate how play supports our grandchildren's development and learning. Lastly, we looked beyond the early years and reaffirmed that play enhances close joyful relationships throughout the years ahead. Although each chapter has a different focus, the theme is the same: *Play supports all aspects of children's development and engenders loving relationships.*

As I wrote the different chapters, I was continually inspired by grandparents' joy in being grandparents, and their insights and wisdom. Grandparents want their style to be in tune with each grandchild, to be observant and listen carefully, to be flexible and responsive. As Linda said, "I'm more relaxed than when I was a parent. I have the luxury of time. I want to do things that are fun. I'm thinking, 'I'm going to focus on you.'"

Whatever our grandchild's age, we grandparents learn so much by talking with each other and sharing our experiences and tips. When we think about how we play, we can see that our play changes with the unique flow and timing of the child's development and changing interests. We each have our own style but we also find commonalities in how we play from, for example, playing peekaboo with infants, to hide and seek with toddlers, to tag with kindergartners.

Sharing stories about play amuses and informs us. The first chapter began with two stories, and it seems fitting that

The Gift of Play concludes with stories. But which ones to choose? Any of dozens of stories would work. As I reread the chapters, I discovered something new in each story.

I encourage you to go back and read the stories for yourself. Were there any stories that you especially related to? Any that brought you particular joy or feelings of tenderness? Any that were quite informative or surprising?

Although it was hard to choose, I selected the following stories—the one of Nick and Marcus from Chapter 1 and the other of Amparo, Levi, and Angel from Chapter 3. At first glance, these stories appear quite different. The children's ages are certainly different. Marcus is 10 months old, while Levi and Angel are older preschoolers. The tempo of play is vastly different as well. Nick takes the lead, and he and Marcus move slowly, almost dreamily, as they quietly reach out to touch the dancing shadows. In contrast, the shadow tag game that Levi, Angel, and Amparo play is boisterous and fast-paced, with lots of running for all three. The children take the lead here. It is Levi who is first intrigued by the shadows, and Angel who comes up with the idea of shadow tag—catching Grandma's shadow.

The two stories have key similarities and not simply because they are both about shadows (which first caught my eye). The grandchildren and grandparents are interested, actively engaged, and having fun. In each case, the pace and tone match the type of play. Emotionally as well as physically, Nick and Amparo are in tune with the children. These two stories, and the many stories in this book, show striking characteristics that symbolize the power and gift of play in grandparent and grandchild relationships.

Outside in the late afternoon, Nick stands under the mulberry tree with Marcus, his 10-month-old grandnephew. Sunbeams reflect off the leaves. The sun hangs low in the sky, half hidden behind the tree and casting shadows against the fence. Moving shadows of leaves on branches flit across the fence. As Nick moves toward the fence, Marcus reaches out to touch the shadow leaves. Nick does the same. Silently, they touch the dancing shadows with their fingers.

Levi and Angel are in the park with Amparo on this sunny late afternoon. Levi stares at his shadow—at least five feet long. Amparo walks over to stand next to him. "Wow, Grandma, your shadow is really, really long!" A few minutes later the children are playing shadow tag on the blacktop of the basketball court, trying to catch the other's shadow with their shadow hand. "Let's play tag," Angel shouts. "Who can catch Grandma's shadow?" Amparo runs across the basketball court and over to the playground. She turns, hiding behind the climbing structure as the boys run after her. Next she runs behind a tree, and then finally sprints for the swings. She sits on a swing, her shadow moving in tandem. Angel reaches her first and touches her shadow shoulder. Amparo holds out an arm. Levi, running right behind, lands on the shadow of her hand. "You both got me!" Amparo exclaims.

THE GIFT OF PLAY

Resources for Grandparents and Families

Chapter 2: Loving Relationships

You can read the two articles I wrote on distance grandparenting in spring 2020 at the links I've provided below. The first is an article for grandparents that appeared in an online edition of *GRAND* magazine. The second article was posted by the nonprofit Defending the Early Years as a resource for parents and families on how to enhance intergenerational relationships during the COVID-19 pandemic. I wrote it with my son Pete, the father of two of my grandchildren, and my colleague Dr. Rebecca Wheat.

Article from *GRAND* Magazine:

Distance Grandparenting with Young Grandchildren

https://www.grandmagazine.com/2020/06/distance
-grandparenting-with-young-grandchildren/

Article from Defending the Early Years:

The Ties That Bind: Forging Loving Relationships Between Children, Parents, and Grandparents During the Pandemic

https://dey.org/the-ties-that-bind-forging-loving-
relationships-between-children-parents-and-grandparents-
during-the-pandemic/

Chapter 3: Grandparents, Grandchildren, and the Development of Play

The Four Dimensions of Temperament and the Implications for Grandparents

by Dr. Ann Sanson

Grandparents with young grandchildren might be more helpful to the child if they're aware of four dimensions of temperament, each along a separate continuum: activity, sociability, reactivity, and regulation.

1. Consider **activity**. Children and their grandparents obviously vary in how physically active they are, how much they need exercise, how long they can sit still on one activity.

2. **Sociability** refers to the tendency to approach new people and situations or to withdraw from them. The highly sociable child will be adventurous, go straight up to new kids in the park, and will be happy going to big parties with people they don't know. Some may put themselves in harm's way by being too outgoing. The very shy child will find all these difficult. They will need time to get used to new situations and people and feel more comfortable in known places. They need more slow, graduated introductions to new experiences—but then are able to make strong relationships.

3. Another dimension is **reactivity**. A highly reactive child will be very responsive to environmental stimulation, like sight, sound, feel, so they respond strongly to experiences (e.g.,

with laughter, crying, lots of movement). Grandparents can anticipate that the child may easily get over-excited and over-aroused—whether with pleasure/joy or distress/anger. On the other hand, grandparents can understand that a very unreactive grandchild will be calm and quiet whatever the situation and may appear rather unresponsive, uninterested, or unimpressionable—unless the grandparent takes the time to understand their subtle communication.

4. **Regulation** refers to the ability to self-regulate emotions and behavior, so it's related to reactivity. Reactive kids have more to regulate than low-reactive kids. Children who are more reactive have a harder time calming themselves down, resisting angry or aggressive outbursts, delaying gratification, etc. In play, very unregulated kids will be impulsive, sometimes appear rude and inconsiderate. On the other hand, very highly regulated kids may be so self-controlled that they don't even recognize their feelings or desires. This aspect of temperament is very amenable to learning and grandparents can help. Over time and with support, preschool and kindergarten-aged children will learn to self-talk to calm themselves down, label their emotions, think of non-aggressive solutions when they're angry, and learn to be patient.

Other aspects of temperament include rhythmicity and activity. Kids vary in the regularity of their biological rhythms (sleep-wake cycles, toileting, feeding, etc.), their ability to sleep and eat at different times and places, etc. And kids obviously vary in how physically active they are, how much they need exercise, how long they can sit still on one activity, etc.

American Academy of Pediatrics' healthychildren.org

https://healthychildren.org/English/Pages/default.aspx

The AAP's website for families, called healthychildren.org, has numerous articles on children's physical, social, language, and emotional development and helpful advice on talking to pediatricians about concerns.

Chapter 4: Play and Language

There are excellent lists of books compiled by expert, noncommercial sources like the American Library Association and the National Association for the Education of Young Children. Many are written by well-loved and prolific authors. Others have won recent awards for children's literature. Look for books you and your grandchild may enjoy that are playful, imaginative, and creative. Check your local library and ask the children's librarian for lists of recommendations.

1. The American Library Association provides a master list of different resources:
    https://libguides.ala.org/recommended-reading/children

2. The National Association for the Education of Young Children, or NAEYC, provides lists of new books, classic books, and lists of books on different topics, such as this list of recommended books for infants and toddlers:
    https://www.naeyc.org/our-work/families/great-books-read-infants-and-toddlers

Chapter 5: Pretend Play

Dr. Diane Levin has written many books. Grandparents find that her books have useful information and advice when thinking about young children's play and development. *So Sexy, So Soon* is written for a wide audience, including grandparents. *Teaching Young Children in Violent Times and Beyond Remote-Controlled Childhood* were written for early childhood educators, but parents and grandparents will find these books both practical and thought provoking.

Chapter 6: The Essential Benefits of Outdoor Play

For important safety tips, read Julie Gilchrist's article "Playground Safety" for the AAP's healthychildren.org:

https://healthychildren.org/English/safety-prevention/at-play/Pages/Safety-on-the-Playground.aspx

Chapter 9: Play, Creativity, and the Arts

Playdough Power

https://www.naeyc.org/our-work/families/playdough-power

You'll find this NAEYC article a powerful resource with recipes and information that will convince you to make playdough a staple for artful explorations and for lots of fun with your grand-child. You may find it hard to choose between the recipes for

"On-Cloud-9-Dough" and "Bouncy Playdough." You'll also want to check out the list of "Around-the-House Playdough Props."

This delightful article also shows how playdough supports children's social and emotional development, creativity and imagination, language and literacy, science and math explorations, and physical development.

Acknowlegments

I've enjoyed writing this book as a collaborative adventure. Above all, I thank the scores of grandparents who shared their stories and sage advice, and the friends and relatives who pored through their photo collections to find playful photos that enliven every chapter. I deeply appreciate your contributions.

I am grateful to many family members, old friends, and colleagues who patiently read drafts of each chapter and encouraged me through the many revisions. As always, Derek is there to cheer me on as my favorite reader and editor. Many thanks to Leni and Hans von Blanckensee, Larry Behrens, Julie Nicholson, Bob Sickles, Victoria Shoemaker, Elizabeth Morley, Elaine and Cooke Sunoo, Linda and Steve Gallon, and to the many others I have thanked personally but who wish to remain anonymous.

This book is the result of my professional as well as personal interest in young children's play. It is influenced by my mentor, Professor Millie Almy, and by Patricia Monighan Nourot, Barbara Scales, and Keith Rodriguez Alward, co-authors of our textbook, *Play at the Center of the Curriculum*.

I gratefully acknowledge the contributions of my colleagues in the fields of early childhood education, psychology, and science education who explained clearly how their specialized knowledge sheds light on multiple dimensions of grandparent and grandchild play: Suzanne Di Lillo, Benina Gould, Linda Kroll, Paula LeVeck, Diane Levin, Larry Malone, Julie Nicholson, Corann Okorodudu, Jane P. Perry, Ann Sanson, Mary Sickles, Dorothy Stewart, Linda Webster, and Rebecca Wheat.

Finally, I want to make a special acknowledgment to Amy Reff, gifted editor and designer extraordinaire, who turned a simple Word file into this beautiful book.

THE GIFT OF PLAY

References

American Association for the Advancement of Science. (1993). *Benchmarks for Science Literacy, Project 2061* (1st ed.). New York, NY: Oxford University Press.

Carson, R. (1965). *The sense of wonder.* New York, NY: Harper & Row.

Dow, C. B. (2015). The power of creative dance. In National Association for the Education of Young Children (Ed.), *Expressing creativity in preschool* (pp. 40–45). Washington, DC: Author.

Gilchrist, J. (2018). *Playground safety.* American Academy of Pediatrics website healthychildren.org. https://www. healthychildren.org/English/safety-prevention/at-play/ Pages/Safety-on-the-Playground.aspx

Kohl, M. A. (2019). Foreword. In J. Van't Hul, *The artful parent* (pp. xi–xii). Boulder, CO: Roost Books.

National Association for the Education of Young Children & National Council of Teachers of Mathematics. (2002, updated 2010). *Early childhood mathematics: Promoting good beginnings* (Position Statement). Washington, DC: National Association for the Education of Young Children. https://www.naeyc.org/sites/default/ files/globally-shared/downloads/PDFs/resources/ position-statements/psmath.pdf

North American Association for Environmental Education. (2016). *Early childhood environmental education programs: Guidelines for excellence.* Washington, DC: Author. https://cdn.naaee.org/sites/default/files/final_ecee_guidelines_from_chromographics_lo_res.pdf

Paley, V. G. (2004). *A child's work: The importance of fantasy play.* Chicago, IL: The University of Chicago Press.

Perry, J. P., & Branum, L. (2009). "Sometimes I pounce on twigs because I'm a meat eater": Supporting physically active play and outdoor learning. *American Journal of Play, 2*(2), 195–214.

Sobel, D. (2008). *Children and nature: Design principles for educators.* Portland, ME: Stenhouse Publishers.

Van Hoorn, J., Nourot, P. M., Scales, B., & Alward, K. R. (2015). *Play at the center of the curriculum* (6th ed.). Boston, MA: Pearson, Inc.

Van't Hul, J. (2019). *The artful parent.* Boulder, CO: Roost Books.

About the Author

The Gift of Play links Dr. Judith Van Hoorn's personal passion with her professional expertise. As an educator, she first became intrigued with young children's play when she worked for the Head Start program in the 1970s. Since then, as a professor, and now professor emerita, at the University of the Pacific, she has written and co-authored numerous books and articles on play for early childhood educators, including *Play at the Center of the Curriculum*, the international bestselling textbook on play, now in its sixth edition, and *Looking at Children's Play*.

Judy has been an invited speaker on children's play at international, national, and state conferences. She is a founding member of the Play, Policy, and Practice Caucus of the National Association for the Education of Young Children, a Fellow of the American Psychological Association (APA), and a recipient of the APA Presidential Citation given to outstanding psychologists. She's an active member of Defending the Early Years and Global Grandmothers, groups that work to improve the lives of young children and their families.

Judy's favorite times are those spent playing with her four active grandchildren and their families. Her grandchildren range in age from 3 to 19 years old, so she gets to play pretend and build with blocks with the younger ones but also gets to hike, cook, and joke around with teenagers—and sing and dance with all four grandchildren.

CPSIA information can be obtained
at www.ICGtesting.com
Printed in the USA
FSHW020440020221
78237FS